MW00658241

PRAYER IN THE
UNSEEN WARFARE

by Jack N. Sparks

a companion volume to
VICTORY IN THE UNSEEN WARFARE
and
VIRTUE IN THE UNSEEN WARFARE

PRAYER IN THE UNSEEN WARFARE

by Jack N. Sparks

adapted and arranged from the classic work
by Lorenzo Scupoli, *Spiritual Combat,*
as edited by Nicodemus of the Holy Mountain
and again by Saint Theophan the Recluse

ANCIENT FAITH PUBLISHING
Chesterton, Indiana

PRAYER IN THE UNSEEN WARFARE
© 1996 Jack N. Sparks

Printed in the United States of America

Published by
Ancient Faith Publishing
P.O. Box 748, Chesterton, Indiana 46304

ISBN: 978-1-888212-03-7

Library of Congress Cataloging-in-Publication Data

Sparks, Jack N.
    Prayer in the unseen warfare / by Jack N. Sparks
        p.   cm.
    "Adapted and arranged from the classic work by Lorenzo
Scupoli, Spiritual combat, as edited by Nicodemus of the Holy
Mountain and again by Saint Theophan the Recluse."
    Includes index.
    ISBN 1-888212-03-9 (pbk)
    1. Spiritual life—Orthodox Eastern Church. 2. Prayer—
Orthodox Eastern Church. 3. Spiritual warfare. 4. Orthodox Eastern
Church—Doctrines. I. Scupoli, Lorenzo, 1530–1610. Combattimento
spirituale. II. Title.
BX382.S637 1997
248.4'819—dc21   96-37840
                                                   CIP

ACKNOWLEDGMENTS

This volume is primarily based upon
selected chapters from:
Spiritual Combat
by Lorenzo Scupoli
as edited by Nicodemus of the Holy Mountain
and revised by Theophan the Recluse

I have worked for the most part from the translation
by E. Kadloubovsky and G.E.H. Palmer, first published
in England in 1952 by Faber and Faber under the title
Unseen Warfare, and later published in the United States
by Saint Vladimir's Seminary Press.

—Jack N. Sparks, Ben Lomond, California, 1996

TABLE OF CONTENTS

An Essential Preface 5
Building on Our Baptism / 6
A Brief History of this Work / 7

Chapter 1
Beginning to Pray 11
The Proper Attitudes for Prayer / 11
STUDY QUESTIONS / 20

Chapter 2
Mental or Inner Prayer 21
What Is Mental Prayer? / 21
Learning to Pray from the Spirit and the Heart / 23
STUDY QUESTIONS / 33

Chapter 3
On Various Forms of Prayer 35
On Praying in Our Own Words / 35
On Short Prayers / 39
On the Jesus Prayer / 42
STUDY QUESTIONS / 50

Chapter 4
The Habit of Prayer in the Unseen Warfare 51
Acquiring the Habit of Prayer / 51
The Role of Prayer in Unseen Warfare / 55
STUDY QUESTIONS / 59

Chapter 5
Fasting, Alms, and Prayer 60
Fasting and Prayer / 60
Giving: Tithes, Alms, and Prayer / 67
STUDY QUESTIONS / 73

Chapter 6
Personal and Corporate Prayer 74
Praying Together and Praying Alone / 75
Lord, Teach Us to Pray / 79
STUDY QUESTIONS / 89

Chapter 7
The Holy Sacrament of the Eucharist 90
Essential Qualities of the Eucharist / 90
The Other Sacraments / 103
STUDY QUESTIONS / 106

Chapter 8
The Eucharist in the Life of Prayer 107
Preparing to Receive the Eucharist / 107
Kindling Love for God through the Eucharist / 112
STUDY QUESTIONS / 122

Chapter 9
On Spiritual Communion and Thanksgiving
to God 123
Communion with the Lord in the Spirit / 123
On Giving Thanks to the Lord / 126
STUDY QUESTIONS / 130

Index 131

AN ESSENTIAL PREFACE

The book you are holding contains essential information for all Christians. Its use, however, requires a context: the Church and Orthodox spiritual guidance. No one should undertake to follow all that is said here without guidance. Everyone needs a spiritual father or guide.

A first reading of this volume can be puzzling. In one sense, it starts from the beginning, as if the reader were just beginning to inquire about following God. However, the content is so deep that any Christian, at any point in life, can receive help from starting at the beginning. And in another sense, this book is only for those who have become so serious about knowing God that everything else pales in comparison.

This is partly due to the fact that Scupoli's *Spiritual Combat* (first published in 1589) and the editions of *Unseen Warfare* which were developed from it came into being within a monastic context. The book is, therefore, a distillation of ascetic spiritual experience. Though the principles of spiritual warfare involved are the same for monastics and laity, there must undoubtedly be adaptations in application, for these are different kinds of lives. It is not our intent to replace *Spiritual Combat* or *Unseen Warfare* in their monastic application, but rather to produce a work which will be of assistance to lay Christians in developing their life with God.

BUILDING ON OUR BAPTISM

Yes, the work developed in a monastic context, where the only aim is to know God and become like Him. But there, at that exact point of entry, we also encounter its application to the life of every Christian.

Our baptismal vows amount to a total commitment to Christ, and it is to these vows, in fact, that the monastic pledge refers. In the Eastern Orthodox tradition, when we come for baptism, we are first asked: "Do you renounce Satan and all his works, and all his worship, and all his angels, and all his pride?" Three times this question is asked, and three times we answer, "I do."

Then we are asked, "Have you renounced Satan?" Again, this question is asked three times, and three times we reply, "I have." We are asked to blow and spit upon Satan, and we do so. Next, we are asked, "Do you unite yourself to Christ?" This question is also asked three times, and three times we commit ourselves to Him: "I do." Immediately we are asked, "Have you united yourself to Christ?" And we emphatically reply, "I have." Finally, we are asked, "And do you believe in Him?" Our answer is, "I believe in Him as King and God." This we follow by repeating the Nicene Creed.

I mention these baptismal vows so we may see that at our baptism we committed ourselves absolutely to Christ, to unite ourselves to Him, to believe in Him as King and God. No greater commitment is possible. But what does it mean to make this commitment?

At the time of our baptism we probably know very little about how it can be practically worked out in our lives. (If baptized as infants, of course, we have extremely little rational knowledge.) But we learn this step by step, if we follow Him. Once we begin to do so, our interaction with His commands, as given in the Sermon on the Mount, for example, is neverending.

That is what this volume is all about—progress in our life with Christ. We cannot do it alone or outside the Church. For we need the Holy Mysteries, the wisdom of the Holy, Catholic, and Apostolic Church communicated to us through the guidance of our fathers, the companionship and encouragement of our brothers and sisters, and all the prayers of the faithful.

Consequently, the task set forth in this book must be seen as lifelong. That which cannot even be comprehended, let alone accomplished, at one stage in our spiritual journey will beckon us along sometime later. One thing we can do is to keep this volume, along with our Bible and prayer book, with us at all times, referring to it often, trusting that it will be continually useful—and that those parts which do not make sense or cannot be undertaken now will perhaps, at some time in the future, have their day in our lives.

A BRIEF HISTORY OF THIS WORK

As was noted, this work derives from a classic of ascetic theology first published by the Italian monk, Lorenzo Scupoli, in 1589, as *Spiritual Combat*. The first edition, published in Venice, consisted of just twenty-four chapters, but successive editions were enlarged to first thirty-three, then thirty-seven, forty, and sixty-six chapters. During the seventeenth century, editions were published under the name of John of Castanzia, a Spanish Benedictine monk. From the content, it is obvious that more than one man was involved in the book's development, and that it is a distillation of Christian ascetic spirituality.

During the latter half of the eighteenth century, an Orthodox monk on Mount Athos, one Nicodemus (now called Nicodemus of the Holy Mountain), began translating *Spiritual Combat* into Greek, making adaptations and changes for the use of Orthodox Christians, adding, as he went, illustrations from the Scriptures and the writings of the Fathers. Among the monks on Mount Athos and among the people of the Orthodox Church in Greece, the adaptation, titled *Unseen Warfare,* became widely read and applied.

Later, in the nineteenth century, a copy of the Greek edition produced by Nicodemus came into the hands of Bishop Theophan the Recluse, a highly respected Russian theologian and spiritual director. Theophan translated *Unseen Warfare* into Russian, making additional changes he felt necessary for the benefit of the people with whom he worked. As a consequence, the work became widely distributed, read, and used in Russia, especially in the monasteries, but among the general populace as well.

The volume you see before you is offered as a modern adaptation of selected portions of this spiritual classic. Though in its preparation I have made use of the English translation of Scupoli's *Spiritual Combat* made in 1945 by

William Lester and Robert Mohan, and published by Tan Books in 1990, I have paid closer attention to the translation of Theophan's Russian edition of *Unseen Warfare* by E. Kadloubovsky and G.E.H. Palmer, published by Faber and Faber of London in 1952 and later republished in the United States by St. Vladimir's Seminary Press.

In addition, I have reorganized the material, combining chapters where appropriate, and arranging the content into three thematic divisions. (This volume represents only one third of the entire work. The other divisions cover victory and virtue.) Like all previous editors of this work, I have incorporated some additional material. I have also added questions for thought or discussion at the end of each chapter. Though this work is designed primarily for personal study and use, I believe significant value can be gained from its use by small groups studying together. Therefore the questions are so constructed that they may be used either as personal study guides or as means of entering into group discussions.

CHAPTER 1

Beginning to Pray

In the two previous volumes (*Victory in the Unseen Warfare* and *Virtue in the Unseen Warfare*), we have discussed three things which are essential to our spiritual warfare: refusing to rely on ourselves, trust in God, and constant effort. In this volume, we will discuss the fourth and most important weapon of all: prayer. Through prayer we are enabled to acquire the first three weapons and use them to their fullest. Further, through prayer we obtain every other blessing of God.

THE PROPER ATTITUDES FOR PRAYER

Prayer is both the means for attracting, and the hand that receives, all the blessings God pours out upon us from the inexhaustible supply of His infinite love and goodness. In spiritual warfare, it is by prayer we put our weapons in the hand of God, so He fights our enemies and overcomes them. But in order for prayer to manifest its full power in us, it must become our constant companion, a natural activity of our spirit. In addition, we can protect and inspire this activity of prayer within our spirit by cultivating the following attitudes.

Struggle to Serve God

Always maintain an enthusiastic struggle to serve only

God in all we do, and to serve Him in a manner acceptable to Him.

In order to establish this tendency and keep it alive, we must have (and always keep in mind) the conviction that every reasoning creature should give the Lord worship, praise, and service. His divine and sacred qualities—His goodness, greatness, and wisdom, as well as His other innumerable and immeasurable perfections—are certainly in themselves sufficient reason for us to do this! Then, we may add to this a constant remembrance that, in an indescribable way, He Himself served and helped us through all He did in His Incarnation: redeemed us; freed us from the great curse of the Fall; ministered to the wounds caused by the poison of sin and healed them—not with medicine of any kind, but with the precious blood which flowed from His most holy side and with His holy flesh tortured by whippings, thorns, and nails. When we remember all this, how can we fail to zealously dedicate to His service every moment of our life, by word, thought, and deed? Furthermore, we must not forget the benefit we receive from such a service, since it makes us masters of ourselves, conquerors of the devil, and children of God.

Have Faith in His Blessings

Maintain a warm and living faith that God Himself, in His great mercy and lovingkindness, wishes and is ready to give us all that is needed for us to serve Him properly—and to bestow upon us every blessing we need. Such faith will become for us a container into which God will pour all the treasures of His blessings. And the bigger the container, the more our faith and trust, the richer will be the gifts which our prayer will carry back to that which is deepest within us. For how could we imagine that the almighty and unchanging God—who commanded us to pray to Him and promised to give us the blessings we ask—would refuse them to us, or that He would not send us His Spirit when we diligently and patiently ask Him?

Desire the Will of God

Approach prayer with the attitude that we desire only the will of God, not our own—both in asking and in receiving what we have asked. Let us, in other words, be moved to prayer because God wishes us to pray; let us wish to be heard because He wishes to hear us. In summary: We must steer our mind and heart to completely unite our will with the will of God—to obey His will in everything, and in no way to desire to bend God's will toward our own.

Why should we approach prayer in this manner? Because our will is always mixed with self-love, is very often mistaken, and does not know what it should wish for. The will of God, on the other hand, is always good, wise, just, and beneficial, and will never lead us astray. Since God's will is an unchangeable law for all that is and will be, obedience to that rule must be central for us all—to be followed submissively in all things.

Consequently, we must always desire, ask for, and seek only what is acceptable to God. And if we are in doubt as to whether one thing or another is acceptable to Him, let us pursue it and ask for it, with the thought that this is what we wish to do or to have—if God also desires it. As to things we are sure are acceptable to God, such as virtue, let us also pursue and ask for them only in order to please God more and serve Him better—and for no other purpose, even a spiritual one.

Work for What You Pray for

Furthermore, we should come to prayer bringing deeds and works corresponding to what we ask. Then after prayer, let us work still harder to become worthy to receive the grace and virtue we are asking for. Thus, the work of prayer should be accompanied by self-motivated action and exertion of all our strength toward what we ask. In the pattern of spiritual life, asking for something and going after it with our own efforts follow one another in an alternating pattern. So if we pray to God for some virtue and then carelessly neglect to pursue it—neither using nor acquiring any definite means to gain this virtue, making no effort in that direction—then we are tempting God rather than praying. That is why we read: "The effective, fervent prayer of a righteous man avails much" (James 5:16).

What serves to make prayer effective, according to Saint Maximus the Confessor, is (in addition to asking a saint to pray for us about it) to pray about it ourselves, industriously doing everything we can to obtain the results of our request.

Include the Four Elements of Prayer

Let us combine in our prayer the four actions Saint Basil the Great describes:

- first, glorify God;
- then give thanks to Him for the mercies He has shown us;
- confess our sins and transgressions of His commandments;
- and finally, ask Him to grant what we need—particularly in regard to our salvation.

In line with this, we might, for example, pray in this manner:

> O Lord my God! I sing and praise Your inexpressible glory and Your infinite greatness. I thank You that by Your goodness alone You have given me life and allowed me to share in the life-giving blessings of Your Incarnation. I thank You that You have often, even without my knowledge, saved me from catastrophes which threatened me, and delivered me from the hands of my unseen enemies. I confess I have, time after time, stifled my conscience and fearlessly transgressed Your holy commandments, showing myself ungrateful for Your many and varied gifts and generous helps. O my most merciful Lord, do not let my lack of gratitude and appreciation be too great for Your mercy, but overlook my sins and transgressions. Look with kindness on the tears of my repentance, and according to what is needed for my salvation, guide my life toward pleasing You, so that, unworthy as I am, I too may glorify Your Holy Name.

At the end of this prayer, it is also appropriate and right to tell all our present needs—those of the spirit, those of the soul, and those of the body. And if we happen to be working on building up some particular virtue, let us mention it as well, praying for God's help in making progress toward perfection in it. Also, if we are being bothered and distressed by some passion, the proper thing is to pray for help in resisting and overpowering it. If we are suffering some injustice, some mistreatment, undergoing a loss or hardship, let us not forget to give thanks to God for it—since being sent in accordance with His will, which is always good, this experience has come for our own benefit.

Pray with Faith—and the Help of the Saints

In order to make our prayer effective before God, attracting His generosity, it is our duty to adorn it and give it wings by a pure faith—not only in His infinite generosity and the unchangeable truth of His promise to hear us when we call to Him, even before our prayer is ended (cf. Isaiah 58:9), but most of all in the power of the special dispensation of our Lord Jesus Christ, who assumed flesh for our sake, suffered death on the Cross, was resurrected, ascended to heaven, and sits at the right hand of the Father, where He unceasingly intercedes for us. For "He who did not spare His own Son, but delivered Him up for us all, how shall He not with Him also freely give us all things?" (Romans 8:32).

For further assistance (for we always need all the help we can get), let us also offer the intercessions of the

Holy Mother of God, the Virgin Mary, who prays for us day and night, and of all the saints; of archangels and angels, apostles and prophets, shepherds and teachers, together with the martyrs, holy fathers and mothers, and those who have pleased God in every possible way; of our guardian angel and our patron saint, and the saints to whom are dedicated the churches in which we were baptized and in which we pray.

By prefacing our prayer with these intercessions, we preface it with humility, which is, of all things, most pleasing to God, for He looks upon no one with more lovingkindness than the person who is meek and humble. "A broken and a contrite heart—these, O God, You will not despise" (Psalm 51:17).

Be Persistent in Prayer

Our prayers are always to be said with tireless persistence—as the Apostle Paul directs, saying: "Continue earnestly in prayer, being vigilant in it with thanksgiving" (Colossians 4:2). For, mystically and in a way we do not understand, humble patience, tirelessness, and persistence in prayer conquer the unconquerable God and incline Him to mercy.

We recall the Lord's parable of the insistent requests of the widow who, by her persistence, caused a wicked and unjust judge to grant her petition: "And he would not for a while; but afterward he said within himself, 'Though I do not fear God nor regard man, yet because this widow troubles me I will avenge her, lest by her continual coming she weary me'" (Luke 18:4, 5). The

Lord gave us this parable for a special purpose—to teach us not to become weary and give up, but to pray patiently, as He said: "Then He spoke a parable to them, that men always ought to pray and not lose heart" (Luke 18:1). If, as we have seen, an unjust judge was persuaded to grant the petition of the widow because she was so persistent, how can God fail to incline His ear to our prayers if we persist in imploring Him—since He is the very essence of lovingkindness?

Therefore, when we beg God to grant us something and He seems slow in hearing us, let us continue to pray, keeping firm trust in His help alive in our heart. For diligent prayer is never left unrewarded by God, and He is always ready to pour out rich blessings in return. These blessings will far exceed the expectations of those who pray, if they have no inner obstacles and are not in a condition such that it is better for them that their petition should remain unfulfilled. In this case, God sends them, instead of what they ask, some other good, more profitable for them (whether they are aware of it or not).

Consequently, we can see that the confidence that prayer never remains unheard is truly justified. What actually happens is this: when we ask, unaware that what we ask is not profitable for us, God does not send what we ask. And what He does send remains unseen, because seeing it can be dangerous for the one who receives it.

Let us, then, always be patient in prayer, convinced that prayer never goes without fruit. If we do not receive what we ask, let us believe we are receiving, or will receive, another good in its place. And if we do not see this good, or come to see it, let us not try to find out why this is so. Rather, let us turn to our own unworthiness and fill our soul with humble thoughts and feelings. If we provoke and encourage such thoughts in ourselves, making them firm and solid as a consequence of prayer, then even if we receive absolutely nothing—visible or invisible—let us accept these feelings themselves as the fruit of prayer, beneficial to ourselves and pleasing to God.

It is profitable for us to listen to some words of Saint John Chrysostom on prayer:

> Prayer is a great blessing if practiced in a proper inner state and if we teach ourselves to give thanks to God— both when we receive what we ask and when we do not receive it. For when He gives, and when He does not give, He does it for your good. Thus, when you receive what you ask, it is quite clear you have received it; but when you do not receive it, you also receive, because you thus do not receive what is undoubtedly harmful for you. And not to receive what is harmful means to be granted what is useful. So whether you receive what you ask or not, give thanks to God in the belief He would have always given us what we ask were it not often better for us not to receive it.

Let us, then, always pray to God with patience. And let us render thanks to Him for all things, believing and professing our belief that He is good to us—wisely good—and is our loving Benefactor, both when He gives and when He does not give what we ask. Firm in this faith, let us remain humbly obedient to divine Providence, meeting gratefully and gladly everything that happens—pleasant or unpleasant.

STUDY QUESTIONS

1. *Write down the content or outline of your present "rule of prayer"—the pattern of prayer you ordinarily follow. Consider (preferably in consultation with your spiritual guide or father) how it might be improved.*
2. *How do you believe you can implement in your life the recommendations given under the first four subheads in this chapter? (Try to tackle them one at a time.)*
3. *How could you integrate the recommendations of Saint Basil into your present rule of prayer? Or, if they are already there, how are they incorporated?*
4. *How do you enumerate your present needs within your present rule of prayer? Are there ways this chapter leads you to make changes in that aspect? What are they?*
5. *Of all the recommendations given in this chapter, which seem most important and practical to you?*

CHAPTER 2

Mental or Inner Prayer

WHAT IS MENTAL PRAYER?

We practice mental prayer when we collect our spirit in our heart and send out our prayer to God from there—not aloud, but in silent words: praising and thanking Him, confessing our sins to Him with repentance, and pleading with Him for blessings for our spiritual and bodily needs.

We are called upon to pray not only in words, but in our spirit, and not only in our spirit, but also in our heart—so our mind sees and understands clearly what is said in words, and our heart feels what our mind thinks. All this, joined together, is real prayer. And if our prayer does not have all this, it is either imperfect or not prayer at all. That fact should, however, not discourage us, but help direct us on our way, for we are, after all, on a journey to God.

We have all probably heard the expressions "prayer with words," "prayer with the spirit," "prayer with the heart," and we may have heard explanations of each of them separately. But why make such a division of prayer into its component parts? For one thing, because of our carelessness and lack of attention, our tongue sometimes says the holy words of prayer while our spirit wanders away somewhere. Or our spirit understands the words of prayer, but our heart does not respond to them with feeling. In the first case, prayer is merely words, and not properly prayer at all. In the second, prayer with words is connected with inner prayer, but it is still flawed—incomplete—prayer. Real and full prayer takes place when our praying words and praying thoughts combine with praying feelings.

There also exists (by the grace of God) prayer of the heart alone. This is called "spiritual prayer"—prayer which the Holy Spirit moves in our heart. The one who prays is conscious of it, but does not do it, for it acts on its own. This is the prayer of the perfect, and most of us do not reach that level. But the form of prayer always attainable to all of us is that form in which spirit and feeling are combined with the words of prayer.

We must add, however, that there is yet another form of prayer—called "standing in the presence of God." This form occurs when the one who prays is wholly and completely concentrated in his heart and inwardly contemplates God as being present to him and within him. This prayer is accompanied by feelings of fear of God, wonder and awe before His greatness, or of faith and hope, or of love and submission to His will, or of repentance and readiness to make any sacrifice.

Such a state of prayer comes when a person becomes deeply immersed in prayer by word, spirit, and heart. If we pray in the right way—and for a long time—this state will come to us more and more often. And it can even finally become permanent. This is called "walking before God" and is equivalent to constant prayer. David was in this state when he said of himself, "I have set the

LORD always before me; because He is at my right hand I shall not be moved" (Psalm 16:8).

Therefore, if we want our prayer to be very fruitful, we must learn never to be content with oral prayer alone. We must work and learn to pray with our heart and spirit as well—using our mind to understand and to be conscious of all that is said in words, and using our heart to feel it all. Above all, we must learn to pray with our heart—and practice it. Prayer bursting from the heart is like a streak of lightning—as if taking but a moment to cross the heavens and appear before the throne of the all-merciful God (of course it is really even faster than that, for we pray right before His throne). Hearing such a prayer, God is especially moved by it. This was, for example, the prayer with which Moses prayed standing before the Red Sea. Immediately he heard God's voice: "Why do you cry to Me?" (Exodus 14:15). And we know God gave him the power to free his people from the danger which threatened them at the hands of Pharaoh and his army. We, too, may expect such action from God when we pray from our heart.

LEARNING TO PRAY FROM THE SPIRIT AND THE HEART

Having gone this far, we should all be ready to ask: How can I learn to pray this way? The answer is: Train yourself. You can train yourself to pray in exactly the way we have described—that is, not only in words, but also in spirit and heart. Train yourself and you will learn. How did you learn to read? Though you had teachers, the fact is, you began to work at it and you did learn. How did you learn to write? You began to write, and you learned. That is also how we learn to pray in the manner set forth—by beginning to pray in exactly this way.

Morning and Evening Prayers

The Church provides ordered forms of morning and evening prayers (most of which are ancient) for the use of her people. These are not exhaustive, but do provide an elementary guide—to be supplemented by prayers we add as our life with God progresses. The main emphasis in prayer, however, is not on the saying of the words, but on our own spiritual concentration.

The ancient Canonicon, the collection of prayers for our personal use upon which our prayer books are based, reads, "Before you begin the day after waking up, stand reverently before the All-Seeing God. Make the Sign of the Cross and say, 'In the Name of the Father and of the Son and of the Holy Spirit, Amen.' Having thus invoked the Holy Trinity, remain silent for a time, freeing your thoughts and feelings from all worldly cares. Then recite the following prayers deliberately and wholeheartedly."

In this instruction (which is directly followed by the morning rule) we immediately see two things:

1) spiritual attention and concentration; and

2) specific Christian doctrinal emphasis from the very beginning: invocation of the Holy Trinity, and the sign of the Cross, pointing to the mystery of our redemption.

We should make no attempt at ecstasy or emotion.

Our perspective should instead be stillness and quietness.

Though you may not realize it, you probably already know the words of prayer. They are to be found in the prayer books and service books of the Church. We also find them in the prayers poured out of the hearts of saintly men and women when, moved by the Holy Spirit, they expressed before God the desires of their hearts. The spirit of prayer is contained in these words. So, if we read them as we should, we too will be filled with this spirit—just as the spirit of a writer is communicated to one who reads with complete attention and absorption. We have all experienced this at one time or another.

These words of prayer are collected in many prayer books, so we do not have to work at gathering them together. Therefore: get yourself a prayer book.

Using a Prayer Book

How, then, shall we proceed? Open your prayer book. Begin by studying the text of the prayers. Then read them before God, meditating on the meaning of each word. Yes, you may, as we have said, do this for months and years, feeling nothing. But be certain: God hears you. Then one day the Holy Spirit Himself will stop you in the middle of the prayers and pray in you, for "the Spirit also helps in our weaknesses. For we do not know what we should pray for as we ought, but the Spirit Himself makes intercession for us with groanings which cannot be uttered" (Romans 8:26).

When He does, it is time to stop speaking, listen to Him, and be led. The purpose of personal worship is to set aside all our self-centeredness and become a vehicle of the Spirit. But that does not mean our individuality— our "personness"—is destroyed. No, it is instead raised to a higher level through communion with the perfect personality of the Holy Spirit.

Thus we see that prayer should not be identified with or equated with petition or request. To pray does not necessarily mean "to ask," although it always means "to seek." "Prayer," writes Saint John of Damascus, "is an ascent to God, or the asking God for things which are fitting." And, of course, there are levels and degrees. We begin with supplication and intercession—laying our needs, defects, and weaknesses before God. He already knows our needs and sorrows much better than we ourselves (Matthew 6:8), but we must ask. And He is always ready to help—even before we ask at all.

Then comes thanksgiving for His divine love. This is, in a sense, a higher level of prayer, leading ultimately to dispassionate praise and adoration of God—while thinking not at all of our needs and problems. In this context of prayer we come face to face with His splendor and glory, to praise Him for His unutterable majesty— the majesty of love that surpasses all knowledge and understanding (see Colossians 1:9; 2:2), not to mention the benefits He imparts to the whole world.

And it is in this sense also that the choir of humanity joins that of the angels, who do not ask or even give thanks at all, but simply praise Him continually for

His eternal glory (1 Peter 5:10), majesty (Jude 25), and splendor, with the words, "Holy, Holy, Holy" (Revelation 4:8). So true prayer is not "me-centered," but God-centered, a glorious ascent from petition to contemplation of the Glory of God.

Then, at the times you fix for prayer (usually in the morning and in the evening), read the prayers you find in your prayer book, paying attention to every word, thinking the thoughts expressed there, and trying to reproduce in your heart the very same feelings stirred up within you when you read the prayer. You must struggle, and will find yourself in a continuing struggle—that is certain, and it will not cease. Christians all over the world do it every day.

Someone might say, "True, many people do this. But if so, why don't they all experience proper prayer?" Because although we do it—that is, we open the prayer book and read—some, perhaps many of us (even all of us at least some of the time), do not bring our whole heart and spirit into it. Our mind wanders in every kind of direction because we don't have it under control. And our heart follows its own pleasure instead of praying.

Therefore, we have an important task before us: we must learn, when we pray, to devote ourselves to making our spirit stick to the words of prayer and making our heart absorb what those words say. When we do that, we will begin to taste the fruit of the words of prayer.

Steps to Success

So we see where we stand: since we have the words

of prayer and know what it means to understand and feel them, the rest depends on us. Prayer and success in it are in our hands. If we work at it diligently, we will succeed. Here are a few pointers which will be helpful in the process:

1) Try to reflect on and feel the prayers you read—not at the hour of prayer, but at some other free time. When we do this, we will have, at the time of prayer, less difficulty reproducing within ourselves the whole content of the prayer we read. We will find that when we read one of our prayers, the thoughts and feelings contained in it will come to our conscious mind, and we will speak the words as if they were truly ours—born in our own heart and pouring out of it, instead of having been brought into it.

2) Having thought about and felt the prayers, try to learn them by heart. Once we have done this, we will carry our prayers around within us. As long as they are only in the prayer book, they are outside us, but when we have learned them by heart, they are within us, so whatever the circumstances, we will always have our prayer book with us. Besides, when we memorize prayers we engrave the praying thoughts and feelings more deeply within ourselves than if we have merely studied them, reflecting so that we felt their meaning. This sort of study of prayers, in which we not only memorize the words but also preserve within ourselves the thoughts and feelings they contain, will help us build a structure of prayer within. It is, in fact, the best method of forming the habit of proper prayer.

3) When it comes time to say your prayers, don't begin to say them just as soon as you have torn yourself away from whatever you happened to be doing just before. Instead, first prepare yourself: stand in silence for a while, to give your heart, spirit, and body a chance to calm down.

Meanwhile, remember what you are about to approach, what you are about to do, who you are who are about to pray, who He is before whom you are about to say your prayers, and exactly what you are going to say, and how.

This sort of preparation is necessary because in the morning our soul is still heavy from sleep, and the cares of the day before us always flood in upon us when we awaken; and in the evening we are full of all the experiences of the day, especially those which stand out as either particularly pleasant or particularly unpleasant.

As we begin, then, we must try to sweep all these things out of our consciousness, so the work of prayer occupies our full attention—and we can devote the time before us exclusively to prayer. If something clings to our consciousness and we cannot succeed in dealing with it, that matter should be turned into a subject for prayer or thanksgiving. In some such cases we may need to ask for help and liberation—or commit them, ourselves, and all we have to God's will. We are there, after all, to deal with our life before Him.

4) Then, just before you begin to say your prayers, bring to your consciousness the feeling and sense that you are standing in the presence of God with reverent

awe. And bring to life in your heart the faith that God sees and hears you—He does not turn away from those who pray to Him, but looks on them with compassion, and He looks upon you now as you pray. Let your prayer be lifted up with hope that He is ready to grant—and will actually grant—your requests that are good for your soul.

5) Now, having brought yourself to this point, say your prayers with the greatest possible attention, taking care to make them come from your heart—as truly your own—even though you have them memorized. We must not let our attention wander off, nor our thoughts begin to roam around. As soon as we notice anything like this happening, we must bring our thoughts back within and resume our prayers from the point at which our attention strayed to something else. Again, we must remember: our attention will not stray when our heart is filled with feelings of prayer. Thus, our first concern should be those feelings. Nor should we allow ourselves to hurry in saying our prayers. Rather, we must continue to the end reverently—with patience—as is fitting for any sacred undertaking.

6) It may be that, while you are saying your prayers, some subject of prayer especially touches your heart— capturing your attention as something very important in your present circumstances. When that happens, do not let the moment slip by. Instead, pause and pray in your own words until the need or feeling for prayer about this particular matter has been satisfied.

7) If you set out to practice saying your prayers in

this way, you will gain the spirit of prayer. We need this spirit very much, and we must try to maintain it in force as much as possible. Therefore, do not throw yourself into your daily schedule of activities immediately after your prayers. And never get the idea that once you have gone through your rule of prayer, you have fulfilled your duty to God and can now turn your thoughts and feelings loose. No! Prayer is not a matter of "fulfilling a duty." Morning prayers are just the start of our day. For the rest of the day, try to keep the same attitude and frame of mind and reference—the same spirit—as during your rule of prayer. There are available to us all some helps we can draw on to assist us in doing this.

To succeed, we must never forget we are walking before God, and His hand alone keeps us above the abyss of death. Keeping this in mind, we must do everything, both large and small, in the way God wishes, asking His blessing and doing everything to the glory of His Name.

If we do these things, we will maintain the right state of mind for prayer all the way up to the time of our evening prayers. Then, if we do them in the same manner, we will sleep properly at night. Thus, we will have lived a day and a night, a full twenty-four hours, in a good prayerful state of being. Keeping it up— passing day after day in this manner—we can, in a few months (or perhaps even weeks), see our prayers gain in strength. Then, prayer will constantly burn in our heart like a light that never goes out.

8) There is one more thing to be added: namely,

the necessity for this work of prayer to go on without interruption from the moment it is begun until we achieve some success. But if we pray well today and keep that state of prayer within, and then tomorrow become careless and spend the day scattered, and so on, we will never achieve success in prayer. That is the same as building up and tearing down. In the end, prayer may dry up altogether and our soul will become incapable of it. Having once begun, we must patiently maintain the life of prayer, never weakening nor pandering to ourselves by special dispensations and indulgences.

The Purpose of Training in Prayer

The purpose of our training in the beginnings of prayer is to enable us to enter into a conversation with God. We may pray at any time of the day—for the aim is that prayer become an attitude of our heart and a habit of our soul. We are to feel ourselves continually and permanently in God's presence. Our ultimate goal in life is, of course, to be with God always. When we are, the Holy Spirit speaks in our heart, joyful and burning. All this is, as we see, far from formalism and ritualism.

Still, there is no place for arbitrary improvisation, for it is the Spirit who does the true and proper improvising within us. We must be cautious and patient, however, for this only happens when our soul has been prepared by long and steady spiritual exercise. Our yearning and hoping for the work of the Holy Spirit must be combined with hard work. Prayer is to be the source and center of our spiritual formation.

The Point of Beginning: Faith in Jesus Christ

Prayer is among those activities we find indispensable in attaining this fellowship with the Spirit. Still, we must remember where we start: for we must begin with a true faith in our Lord Jesus Christ, the Son of God, who came into the world to save sinners (1 Timothy 1:15). Through His promise we have access to the Holy Spirit (John 14:16), the Kingdom of God (John 3:3–5), and the blessings of life eternal (John 17:3).

When, then, we pray to the Holy Spirit in our daily prayers, "Come and abide in us, cleanse us from every stain, and save our souls, O Good One," we can be confident of His desire to help us as we labor to experience His presence. For as we said, the search for the Spirit is to be combined with hard work. Nor do we imply that "good works" are means of salvation. There is nothing meritorious about the works we do. They are, instead, fruits of obedience and complete self-dedication to God and His purpose. They are duties, but not virtues. They are our grateful response to the redeeming grace and mercy of the Living God, revealed and outpoured in Jesus Christ, the Lord and Savior of all.

STUDY QUESTIONS

1. *Have you been able to follow the process of collecting your spirit in your heart? If not, what would you say has been the major block in your ability to do so? If so, how has it helped your prayer life and your relationship with God?*

2. *Consider the kinds or levels of prayer discussed in this chapter. What would need to happen for you to experience them? What is the next step you need to take?*

3. *Consider once more the rule of prayer you presently follow. What would you now say about its effectiveness for you?*

4. *What elements of this chapter seem to be of most value to you in improving your prayer life? What was the most striking part of the presentation?*

5. *How do you believe you can immediately improve your prayer life?*

CHAPTER 3

On Various Forms of Prayer

ON PRAYING IN OUR OWN WORDS

We have written so far of prayers, hymns, and psalms in words already provided—which, though said with attention and feeling, truly coming from our heart, are not words of our own in the sense of being put together by us. But should we always restrict ourselves to these written prayers?

Actually, when we begin to pray, prayer itself will answer this question. Yes, the thing to do is to begin with established prayers—which we will commit to memory as time goes on. This is the proper way to begin, and from doing so we will learn the ways of prayer. When we do so, prayer will, from the very start, begin to graft itself onto our heart. The more firmly it becomes grafted, the more firmly it will urge us to send forth personal prayers, which are formed within our heart according to our needs. We will find ourselves addressing such prayers to God along with our regular rule of prayer. Thus, prayers in our own words have their recognized place and part in the work of prayer.

In the preceding chapter we advised that when, during our prayers, the words of some prayer especially touch our soul and fill it, we must not neglect them. The thing to do is to pause and pray from within our heart about the matter which is filling our soul. The same urge to prayer often happens when we read the Scriptures or the profitable writings of the Holy Fathers, or when we simply meditate on or contemplate holy things: the greatness and perfection of God, His wonderful works of creation, His omnipotence and Providence, and the marvel of His Incarnation to save us.

Sudden Impulses to Pray

We also get such urges to prayer from especially striking and impressive occurrences in our daily life. In other words, something particularly captures the attention of our soul, urging it to ascend in prayer to God. Whenever that happens, we must not neglect the impulse, but immediately respond, interrupting—to pray on this matter—whatever we happen to be doing.

These sudden impulses to prayer are very important for us because they mean prayer has begun to inhabit our heart and to fill it. For they usually do not happen when we first undertake to train our hearts and minds in prayer—they come only after we have worked at it for a while. These impulses to prayer are, in fact, proof of progress in the work of prayer, and the more frequently they come, the more the spirit of prayer fills our heart. Indeed it can happen that eventually we come to the point of always praying in our own words alone. In actual fact it does not happen just that way, but what can happen is that our own prayer enters into the set prayers of our rule. For they are of the same nature and the same degree of virtue, and if they are replaced, it is by standing in the presence of God in wordless contemplation.

Sometimes only the impulse to pray comes to us, but on other occasions prayer itself accompanies the impulse—forming in our heart without effort on our part. In the first case, we must find the words for a suitable prayer, but in the second, we must simply listen, not interfering with the prayer pouring from our heart. That also brings up another important matter: we must not be tempted by the desire to formulate our own prayers without such inner impulses and necessity. We can compose very clever speeches to God which are not prayer, but merely combinations of words and thoughts, lacking the spirit of prayer. Therefore, we must not do this. It leads to a spirit of pride and a high opinion of ourselves—attitudes which stifle and stamp out real prayer.

As regards prayer that forms within our heart, when the urge arises in our heart to pray about something affecting us personally—something we especially need—very often that prayer is actually our own creation from the elements of prayer, collected within our heart from learning and assimilating existing prayers. Sometimes, however, it is produced directly by the action of divine grace. In such cases, it is the seed and germ of the spiritual prayer we mentioned in Chapter 2. When we begin to be granted this, it will mean we are approaching the boundaries of the perfection accessible to us. Then we must give thanks to God and walk on the path of life with still greater fear and trembling. The more precious the treasure, the more covetous the eyes of our enemies become to possess us.

We've already noted: real prayer is inner prayer, carried out not only in words, but with our spirit and heart taking part as well. This kind of prayer captures our whole attention and keeps it within—in our heart. Consequently, remaining within—in our heart—is an absolute necessity for, and the main condition of, real prayer.

Guarding the Heart

The thought of God as being present and listening to our prayer, along with the rejection of every other thought, is inseparable from remaining within in our prayer. This is commonly called "guarding the heart." Therefore, our efforts must be primarily directed toward achieving this purpose, never deviating from it: never to leave our heart, soberly protecting it from every thought except the thought of God alone. Along with that thought, we must so focus ourselves as to do whatever we have to do without turning away from this thought of God, maintaining our consciousness of His presence—as though we were before His Face. We must recognize and accept this to be the highest, the most significant, aspect of the work of prayer.

Saying our prayers in the manner we have indicated above is the way to achieve this result—and is truly the way for us to realize the necessity for it. Teaching our spirit to concentrate on our heart is directly coupled with giving attention exclusively to God. Once we have learned the value of this concentration, it becomes natural to want it to become a permanent condition of our spirit—for then we would have constant prayer—and that desire will lead us to efforts to attain it. This is the direction in which the instructions of the Holy Fathers on guarding the heart lead—and these instructions spring from their achievements in this vital spiritual work.

ON SHORT PRAYERS

When we feel the need for such prayer, we will ask: How can I achieve this constant abiding within, before God's face, accompanied by a sober guarding of my heart? We reach it step by step:

1) Beginning to say our prayers opens the way and produces the beginnings, but it does not reach the end itself—does not bring it to the required strength and perfection. The saying of prayers is a complex activity, with many ramifications. It contains and offers to our attention many subjects which, although holy, may remind us of others belonging to our daily life or our social activities. Through these things brought to our attention in the saying of our prayers, we may be led (by the usual laws of association of thoughts and visualizations) to various worldly and irrelevant subjects.

Thus it happens: even the most diligent rule of prayer can never be practiced without our thoughts darting away and wandering outside. Since this disturbs our prayer and keeps it from being perfect, there is no one who practices prayer and is not distressed by it, wanting to be delivered from this defect.

2) One of the means devised to get around this problem is to say short prayers which keep our thoughts inside, before the face of God, giving them no chance to stray or go outside. Saint John Cassian writes of this practice being general in Egypt in his time (Discourse X, 10). And from the teachings of other Fathers we see it has been used throughout the centuries on Mount Sinai, in Palestine, in Syria, and in fact everywhere in the Christian world. Indeed, what other meaning have the constant cry, "Lord have mercy!" and other short prayers which fill our divine services and our psalmody? Here, then, is good advice:

• Choose for yourself a short prayer, or several such prayers.

• Repeat this prayer (or these prayers) till you reach a point at which they go on repeating themselves on your tongue.

• In the meantime, keep your thought focused on just one thing: remembrance of God.

3) Naturally, everyone is free to choose his own short prayers. If we read the Psalms, we will find inspiring appeals to God in almost every one of them. So the Psalms represent one very good source. Here is what to do:

• Choose from among the short prayers available to you those most closely related to your state of spirit and heart—and those most appealing to you.

• Learn these appeals or prayers by heart.

• To use these short prayers, repeat now one, then another, then a third.

- Intersperse your saying of your prayer rule with these.
- Also keep these short prayers in mind so they are on your tongue at all times, whatever you are doing, from one set time of prayer to another.

4) It is also appropriate to formulate our own short prayer appeals if something comes to mind better expressing our need—wording them on the model of the twenty-four prayers constructed by Saint John Chrysostom.

But do not select too many different prayers. To do so both overburdens our memory and allows our attention to run back and forth among them—a result totally contrary to the purpose we set out to achieve: to keep our attention collected. The twenty-four prayers of Saint John Chrysostom constitute a maximum. We can certainly use fewer. It is good to have more than one, for variety and to enliven our spiritual taste, but in using them, do not go from one to the other too quickly. It is best to proceed by taking one which corresponds to our spiritual need, then using it to appeal to God until our taste for it becomes blunted. We can replace all or part of our psalmody by these short prayers. They should, however, be repeated many times—ten, fifty, or a hundred times—with short bows, physical or internal. And we must always keep one thing in mind: holding our attention constantly directed toward God.

These, then, we will call short prayers, sighs to God, continued at all times during the day and night (when we are not sleeping).

ON THE JESUS PRAYER

Throughout the centuries there have been, and still are, people who, in order to maintain a consciousness of God, His presence, and His help, have chosen one particular short prayer, repeating it constantly. Saint John Cassian says that the prayer usually repeated in his time by everyone in Egypt was the first verse of Psalm 70: "Make haste, O God, to deliver me! Make haste to help me, O LORD!"

In the biography of Saint Joannicius (d. A.D. 846) we are told he repeated the following prayer: "The Father is my hope, the Son is my refuge, the Holy Spirit is my protection." He also added it to each verse of the thirty psalms which he had memorized—and which consti- tuted his rule of prayer. Another holy man is said to have constantly used as his prayer the words, "Being a man I have sinned; but You, being God the Compassionate, have mercy on me."

From the most ancient Christian times, the prayer chosen by many has been: "Lord Jesus Christ, Son of God, have mercy on me, a sinner." Evidence of its use may be found in the writings of Saint Ephraim the Syrian, Saint John Chrysostom, Saint Isaac of Syria, Saint Hesychius, Saint John of the Ladder, and many others. Later it became more and more widely used (with slight variations in wording), and began to be on the lips of people everywhere, throughout the Church. Consequently, we now find it used by more Christians than any other short prayer.

This prayer came to be called "the Jesus Prayer,"

obviously because it is addressed to our Lord Jesus. Like any other short prayer, it is verbal—but it becomes mental when it is said not only in words, but also in the mind and heart, with both consciousness and feeling of its content. Used in this manner, the Jesus Prayer can, first of all, be very helpful in our effort to clear our mind of all external things as we begin our rule of prayer, so we may concentrate on Jesus Christ our Lord, who is our life.

Some people have felt that the words of Christ in Matthew 6:7, 8 prohibit any form of repetitive prayer—including, of course, the Jesus Prayer. That passage reads, "And when you pray, do not use vain repetitions as the heathen do. For they think that they will be heard for their many words. Therefore do not be like them. For your Father knows the things you have need of before you ask Him." Those who object to the Jesus Prayer on these grounds take the phrase "vain repetitions" as their key, tearing it from its context. That, however, is not the meaning of this passage, which should, instead, be taken as an encouragement to use the Jesus Prayer.

In the context of this passage, our Lord is dealing with the problem of spiritual pride—and especially the public display of one's spirituality, which is a certain indication of that pride. If we follow the context, we remember He has just condemned those who said their prayers in public, meaning for others to hear them and look up to them for it, rather than actually speaking to God. Now He attacks a similar practice of certain Gentiles who lived nearby, of publicly petitioning their deities with long lists of requests—with the hope of exhausting the patience of those gods, receiving their desires only because the gods wished to hear them no more. The Lord Jesus is teaching that such things are not necessary when we pray to the True and Living God, for He knows what we need before we ask Him. In the process, and by intention, He reveals the love of God the Father, who wishes to provide for the needs of His children.

[Because of the introduction of various non-Christian religions into American culture, particularly those related to Hinduism—we think immediately of Hare Krishna and Transcendental Meditation—some people have wondered whether the use of the Jesus Prayer might not be similar to such groups' use of a mantra. These religious groups do, of course, engage in various forms of spiritual meditation. In the process, the practitioner is given a short word or phrase (to be his mantra) which is repeated, often for hours on end, with the goal and intent of reaching a state of altered consciousness—a "detachment from the body." The words or phrases making up the mantra usually have very little or no intrinsic meaning, for their only purpose is as a focal point for the mind—a means, therefore, to reach that state of altered consciousness.

These religions are, of course, not Christian. They do not worship the Holy Trinity, nor do they acknowledge Jesus Christ as Son of God and Son of Man. They therefore lead their adherents spiritually astray. They are properly attacked as false. Occasionally, however, people have condemned the Jesus Prayer as being like the mantras used by these religious groups. As a result, some Christians have been confused about its use.

There are, however, significant differences, for the Jesus Prayer is truly a prayer, and the intent of its use is to arouse a constant awareness of the presence of God—not to create an altered consciousness, a mindless euphoria. It is used to enable the Christian to maintain a sure realization and recognition of the majesty of God and our dependence upon His grace. Thus, its repeated use is intended to help focus our mind, so that we can pray without the distractions of our life and environment intruding. Editor's note.]

In the writings of the Holy Fathers, there are many warnings and much advice concerning the use of the Jesus Prayer. All of them are the result of experience— often in carrying out wrong practices. To avoid these faults and others, you need a counselor—your spiritual father—with whom you can talk and verify all that occurs when you use the Jesus Prayer.

We emphasize here that once you enter upon a significant use of this prayer, it is no longer sufficient to go merely to an associate, a friend of the same mind, with whom you can talk. Now you need an experienced spiritual father to verify all that occurs when you use the Jesus Prayer. Always remember, it is not a toy; it must be prayer. Behave and keep yourself in a condition of total simplicity and great humility, never attributing success to yourself. The fact is, true success in prayer comes within, unnoticed, without display or fanfare, just as our physical body grows.

Help from the Fathers

The Holy Fathers offer some additional help concerning further use of the Jesus Prayer. The uses they suggest, however, require (as we have said) the assistance of a spiritual father to whom we look for guidance in prayer. Given that condition and a firm intent on our part to work closely with our spiritual father, we can also apply the Jesus Prayer as follows:

1) This prayer can become a permanent feature of our inner life—and this is especially true if, through long and attentive practice, it becomes so merged with the activity of our spirit that we no longer have to think about the words for the thought to be there.

2) Actually, every short prayer can reach this point. The Jesus Prayer is most prominent, however, because it unites our soul with our Lord Jesus—and the Lord Jesus is the only door to union with God, which is, after all, the aim of prayer. For He Himself said: "No one comes to the Father except through Me" (John 14:6). It is, therefore, no surprise that serious Christians have given themselves over to forming the habit of this prayer.

3) Externally, acquiring the habit of this prayer consists in reaching the point at which it is constantly on our tongue on its own, without our effort. Internally, it consists in concentrating the attention of our spirit in our heart—and in constantly standing there in the presence of the Lord, experiencing varying degrees of heartfelt warmth, rejecting all other thoughts, and above all falling at the feet of our Lord and Savior with repentance and humility.

4) The first step toward this habit is repeating this prayer as often as possible with our attention centered in our heart. Frequent repetition with the right attitude, becoming established, helps us collect our spirit into our heart, standing in the presence of the Lord. When we have established this arrangement within, we are able to experience an accompanying warmth in our heart and a rejection of all external thoughts. Then, clinging to the Lord alone, we can establish peace of heart—with repentant and humble inner prostrations before the Lord.

5) It is only by the help of divine grace that our efforts can ever bring us to this point, but we can never get there without making the effort. If we gain anything more in the work of prayer, it will be a gift of grace alone. The Holy Fathers tell us about this for just one reason: so when we have reached this point, we will not believe we have nothing more to wish for, nor imagine we have reached the very summit of perfection in prayer—or in spiritual achievement.

6) The task at hand, then, is to learn how to properly utilize the Jesus Prayer. You can work on it, under the guidance of your spiritual father, in this manner:

• Reserve a place for the Jesus Prayer in your rule of prayer. At first, repeat this prayer several times at the start of your rule and several times at the end. Later, you might do the same after every prayer in your rule, in the manner of Saint Joannicius the Great, who, after every verse of the psalms included in his rule of prayer, repeated his short prayer: "The Father is my hope, the

Son is my refuge, the Holy Spirit is my protection."

• Determine (with the counsel of your spiritual father) the number of times you should repeat this prayer (and on what occasions). Just remember, however: don't undertake too much at first. Increase the number of repetitions gradually—as your enjoyment of this prayer grows. If, on a particular occasion, you wish to double the set number, do it, but don't set that as a new rule for yourself—just do it this time. In other words (within the limits you and your spiritual father set), whatever number of repetitions your heart desires, do them.

• Don't hurry to go from one prayer to another, but say them with careful deliberation, as you would in making a request from some important human person. And take care not only of the words themselves, but carefully keep your spirit in your heart—standing there before the Lord, as though He were physically present, with full consciousness of His greatness, grace, and truth.

• If, during the day or night, between one of your set times for prayer and the next, you have free time, it may be appropriate to use it to say the Jesus Prayer. Just pause, collect your attention—as you do when you say your regular prayers—and send this prayer to the Lord, repeating it several times. If you have no free time, insert this prayer inwardly wherever you can in the intervals between your activities and duties. Saint John of the Ladder has said, "Let the remembrance of death and the concise Jesus Prayer go to sleep with you and get up with you, for nothing helps you as these do when you are asleep."

•   You may find it appropriate, when you are making this prayer during your rule, or standing in the position of prayer between your regular times of prayer, to make a bow after each repetition.

•   Additional instructions, hints, and warnings about the Jesus Prayer may be found in the *Philokalia*. These are to be seen especially in the works of Simeon the New Theologian, Gregory of Sinai, Nicephorus the Monk, Callistus, and Ignatius. The teachings of all the other Holy Fathers about inner prayer can also (as always, with the guidance of your spiritual father) be applied to the Jesus Prayer. It is for the most part sufficient for us to keep our attention in our heart, before the face of the Lord—and to send Him this short prayer with reverence and humility. Sometimes we may find it proper to use bows if we are standing for our rule, but to use only mental prostrations when we do it during our ordinary activities.

•   Remember: we have said it is good to focus our attention in our heart. Where is that—physically, I mean? No one really knows for sure. Wherever you locate your heart—your inner heart, that is—focus there and repeat the Jesus Prayer in that place.

•   Don't set a time limit for achievement of results with this prayer. Decide just one thing: to work and work. Months and years will often go by before the first feeble indications of true success begin to show. One of the fathers of Mount Athos once said of himself that two years of work passed before his heart grew warm. With each of us results come in accordance with our abilities, our patience, and our diligence in this work.

STUDY QUESTIONS

1. *Have you had experience adding spontaneous prayers to your rule? How did this occur?*
2. *What short prayers, if any, do you use? Why have you chosen those particular ones?*
3. *Do you see the Jesus Prayer as being a short prayer of particular value to you? What first attracted you to it?*
4. *How can you incorporate the Jesus Prayer in your rule of prayer?*
5. *What times during the day can you say the Jesus Prayer without disrupting your duties? In what ways (if any) do you presently see that as helpful?*

CHAPTER 4

The Habit of Prayer in the Unseen Warfare

ACQUIRING THE HABIT OF PRAYER

If we truly desire to pursue success in the work of prayer, we must adapt everything else to this goal. Otherwise we will destroy with one hand what we build with the other. Therefore, to pursue this goal wholeheartedly:

1) Keep your body strictly disciplined in food, sleep, and rest. Don't give it anything simply because it wants it. As the Apostle Paul writes: "Make no provision for the flesh, to fulfill its lusts" (Romans 13:14).

2) Wherever possible, reduce your external contacts to the most inevitable ones. If you must live and work in the world, if you have a family, you must fulfill your duties to those for whom you are responsible. Nevertheless, you must reduce unnecessary contacts with the external world and its influences. Be wise, however, and not selfish. Your spiritual life must not be built at the expense of others whom you must serve, love, and care for. Your spouse and your children (and others for whom you bear responsibility) must not suffer the lack of what you are supposed to give them in order for you to attempt spiritual growth—neglect them and you build nothing. Caring for them properly is, in fact, part of proper Christian living. You must do your work of prayer and build it within the context of

the life situation and position you hold in the world.

As for yourself, watch out! Be careful what you watch (especially theatre and entertainment); be careful what you read (especially novels and all other fiction); watch out for and be very careful about accepting the entertainment offered all around you. Within these categories and others there is more distraction than you can imagine. So restrict yourself. Later, when prayer has begun to act upon you, it will indicate of itself what can be added without harming it. Especially guard your senses—eyes and ears above all. Watch your tongue. Without this guarding you will not make a single step forward in the work of prayer.

3) Use the time you have free from your duties and from your prayer in doing good works and in reading and meditation. For reading, choose, wherever possible, appropriate books dealing with prayer and inner spiritual life. Meditate on God and on divine matters—and above all on the Incarnation of our Lord for our salvation, primarily on His suffering and death. When you do this, you will be immersed in a sea of divine light. In addition, go to church whenever you possibly can. Merely being present there will envelop you in a cloud of prayer. And just imagine what you will then receive if you remain throughout the service in a true state of prayer!

4) We must also learn this and keep it always in mind: it is impossible to make progress in prayer without general progress in Christian living. It is absolutely necessary to make sure no sin not purified by

repentance remains to burden our soul. If, during your work on prayer, you do something which troubles your conscience, hasten to purify yourself by repentance, so you can look up to the Lord boldly. We must keep our hearts humbly repentant and contrite. Furthermore, neglect no opportunity for doing good—or for exhibiting a good, proper, and thoroughly Christian frame of heart, mind, body, and soul. Above all, we must be humble and obedient, bypassing our own will for God's in the service of others. And this goes without saying: Zeal for salvation must always be burning within us and filling our soul—in everything, small and great, it must be the primary motivating force of our lives, along with fear of God and unshaken trust in Him.

5) Having firmly grounded and established yourself in these things, labor diligently at prayer, praying now with the set prayers in your rule, now with those which come to your mind, now with short appeals to the Lord, now with the Jesus Prayer—omitting nothing which can help you in this work. In so doing, you will receive what you seek. We do well to remember the words of Saint Macarius of Egypt: God will see your work of prayer and your wish to succeed in prayer—and will give you prayer. For we must understand: although prayer done and achieved with our own efforts is pleasing to God, that real prayer which comes to dwell in our heart and becomes constant is the gift of God—an act of divine grace. So, in our prayer for everything else, let us not forget to pray about prayer as well.

6) One man who loved God once said:

I was not living a very good life, but God had mercy on me and sent me the spirit of repentance. This was during preparation for communion. I was trying hard to plant in myself a firm resolve to mend my ways, and especially before the icon of the Mother of God I prayed for a long time, asking her to help me obtain this resolve. Then, during confession, I candidly told everything. My spiritual father said nothing about it, but while he was saying the prayer of absolution over my head, a small pleasant flame was lit in my heart. The sensation was like swallowing some delicious food. This little flame remained in my heart, and I felt as though someone was gripping my heart. From that time on I prayed continuously, and kept my attention there, where this sensation was—my only care being to preserve it. And God helped me. I had not heard about the Jesus prayer, and when I did hear of it, I saw that what was within me was precisely that which is sought by this prayer.

This story should help us understand something of what we are pursuing in our work of prayer and what are some of the signs it has been received.

7) Pertinent to our needs are the following words of Saint Gregory of Sinai:

Grace abides in us from the time of our holy baptism; but through our inattention, vanity and the wrong life we lead, it is stifled or buried. When someone resolves to live a righteous life and is zealous for salvation, the fruit of his whole labor is, therefore, the restoration in force of this gift of grace. It comes to pass in a twofold manner: (a) this gift becomes revealed through many labors in following the commandments; in so far as a person succeeds in following the commandments, this gift becomes more radiant and brilliant; (b) it manifests and reveals itself through constant invocation of the Lord Jesus in prayer. The first method is powerful, but the second is more so—thus, even the first method gains power through it. If, then, we sincerely wish to open the seed of grace concealed in us, let us hasten to train ourselves in this latter exercise of the heart, and let us have only this work of prayer in our heart, without forms, without images, till it warms our heart and makes it burn with inexpressible love of the Lord (*Philokalia,* Part I, p. 112).

What more can we say? The words of Gregory support all we have written above.

THE ROLE OF PRAYER IN UNSEEN WARFARE

In writing about prayer, we have focused our attention primarily on the means of raising prayer to the level to which it belongs. It may seem strange that, in writing about unseen warfare (and wanting to show how prayer can help in it), we have dealt so far only with how to make prayer real prayer.

Actually, however, this should not be surprising, for prayer can become a victorious weapon in our unseen warfare only when it becomes real—that is, when it takes root in our heart and begins to act there without ceasing.

From that moment prayer becomes an impenetrable, unconquerable, and insurmountable barrier, protecting our soul from the arrows of our enemy the devil and his demons, the assaults of the passions through the flesh, and the enticements of the world with its delusions.

The very presence of real prayer in our heart brings victory in the unseen warfare. That is why we are advised to move quickly to graft the action of prayer onto our heart—and to see that it remains constantly in action. For this is the same as to say, "Do this and you will conquer"—even without struggle.

And, if we are willing to accept it, this is how it actually happens. But until our prayer becomes so thoroughly real, enemies will give us no peace—and we will not have a single moment of rest from war or threat of war. Does prayer really stifle these attacks? It certainly does!—and more so than any other weapon of spiritual warfare. Prayer always attracts the help of God, and God's power drives back our enemies—as long as it is practiced with zeal and with surrender to God's will. Its place is at the very forefront of our resistance to enemy attacks. This is how such matters should go:

1) When, like a watchful sentry, our attention sounds the alarm about the approaching enemy, and enemy arrows begin to be felt—that is, either a lustful thought or the stirrings of passion appear within—our spirit, aflame with zeal for salvation, recognizes it to be the evildoing of the enemy and, by stretching its powers to the utmost, mercilessly expels it from our heart, not letting it penetrate within.

2) At the same moment, almost as one and the same inner action, our spirit ascends to God in prayer, calling for His help.

3) Help comes, the enemies are dispersed, and the battle subsides.

In a characterization of his own experience, one very godly man describes this process exactly, saying of himself:

> I am like a man sitting under a large tree, who sees a multitude of animals and snakes advancing toward him. He cannot stand up to them, so he hastily climbs the tree and is safe. It is the same with me: I sit in my cell and see evil thoughts rise up against me; since I am not strong enough to resist them, I run to God by means of prayer, and so save myself from the enemy (True Sayings, par. 11).

The Advice of Saint Hesychius

Saint Hesychius writes along the same line in his chapters on prayer and sobriety:

> You should look within with a keen and intense gaze of the spirit, so as to perceive those who enter; and when you perceive them, you should at once crush the head of the snake by resistance; and along with this, call on Christ with groaning. And then you will gain the experience of Divine intercession (*The Philokalia,* Vol. I, p. 165, par. 22).
>
> Every time wicked thoughts multiply within us, let us throw among them the invocation of our Lord Jesus

Christ. Then we shall immediately see them dispersed like smoke in the air—as experience teaches (ibid., p. 179, par. 98).

Let us conduct this mental war in the following order: The first thing is attention; then, when we notice a wicked thought draw near, let us angrily hurl a heartfelt curse at it. The third thing is to turn our heart to call upon Jesus Christ and pray Him to disperse immediately this phantom of the demons, lest our spirit run after this fantasy like a child attracted by a skillful juggler (ibid., p. 180, par. 105).

Opposition usually bars the further progress of thoughts, and invocation of the name of Jesus Christ banishes them from the heart. As soon as a suggestion is formed in our soul by an image of some physical object—such as a man who has wronged us, or a beautiful woman, or silver and gold, or when thoughts of all these things come to us—it immediately becomes clear these fantasies were brought to our heart by the spirits of ill-will, lust and avarice. If our mind is experienced, trained and accustomed to protect itself from suggestions and to see clearly—as if by the light of day—the seductive fantasies and deceptions of the demons, then, by resistance, contradiction, and prayer to Jesus Christ, it immediately and easily repels the red-hot arrows of the devil. It does not allow the fantasies of the passions to entice our thoughts away and forbids our thoughts to attach themselves to the suggested images or to associate with these images and allow them to multiply or to identify with them—for evil deeds follow upon all this as inevitably as night follows day (ibid., pp. 186-187, par. 143).

If we read Saint Hesychius' writings at length, we will find in them many similar passages—and will find he gives a complete outline of all our unseen warfare.

STUDY QUESTIONS

1. *How can you adjust your use of time so you give yourself over to prayer? What activities do you participate in which are detrimental to a proper inner life? Can you eliminate some of them?*
2. *How can you make progress in Christian living?*
3. *What can you find in the story related in (6) above to help guide you in your prayer life? What can you find in the counsel of Saint Gregory of Sinai?*
4. *How have you given attention to making prayer an insepa-rable part of your life? In what ways can the content of this chapter be helpful to you in that task?*
5. *What specific help do you find in the advice of Saint Hesychius?*

CHAPTER 5

Fasting, Alms, and Prayer

FASTING AND PRAYER

Fasting, openhanded giving, and prayer properly and naturally accompany each other. In Israel, fasts were associated especially with times of prayer. The Prophet Joel, for example, in calling Israel to repentance, said, "Consecrate a fast, call a sacred assembly; gather the elders and all the inhabitants of the land into the house of the LORD your God, and cry out to the LORD" (Joel 1:14). Our Lord, when instructing His disciples on prayer, gave that prayer—often called "The Lord's Prayer," and sometimes, "The Our Father"—which we pray so very often. In almost the very same breath, He said, "When you fast..." (Matthew 6:16), giving instructions on what to do and what not to do when fasting. When casting out a demon His disciples were not able to budge, He said, "This kind does not go out except by prayer and fasting" (Matthew 17:21).

It is not surprising, therefore, as we enter the days following His death, Resurrection, and Ascension, to find people who seek Him fasting and praying—as exemplified by Cornelius, who said, "I was fasting until this hour; and at the ninth hour I prayed in my house, and behold, a man stood before me in bright clothing, and said, 'Cornelius, your prayer has been heard, and your alms are remembered in the sight of God'" (Acts

10:30, 31). The combination is especially striking in this instance.

Saint Paul mentions giving oneself to fasting and prayer (1 Corinthians 7:5). Of himself he writes, "We give no offense in anything, that our ministry may not be blamed. But in all things we commend ourselves as ministers of God: in much patience, in tribulations, in needs, in distresses, in stripes, in imprisonments, in tumults, in labors, in sleeplessness, in fastings; by purity, by knowledge, by longsuffering, by kindness, by the Holy Spirit, by sincere love, by the word of truth, by the power of God, by the armor of righteousness on the right hand and on the left. . ." (2 Corinthians 6:3–7).

As we follow the progress of the Church through the centuries, we find fasts observed not only individually, but collectively as well, with days and seasons set aside for fasting. In all this the aim is our spiritual development. Saint Athanasius, writing in his first Easter Letter in A.D. 329, says:

> We are to fast not only with the body, but also with the soul. Now, the soul is humbled when it is not occupied with wicked ideas, but is fed by appropriate thoughts. Virtues and vices are the food of the soul and it can feed on either one, turning to whichever one wants it to. If it is bent toward moral excellence, it will be fed by virtue—by righteousness, temperance, meekness, endurance. In other words, it is just as Saint Paul says, "being nourished by the word of truth" (1 Timothy 4:6). That is the way it was with our Lord, who said, "My

food is to do the will of Him who sent me."

But if the soul does not incline toward good things, but rather toward evil, it is nourished by nothing but sin. The Holy Spirit, describing sinners and their food, alluded to the devil when he said, "You gave him as food for the people of the wilderness" (Psalm 74:14). Our Lord and Savior Jesus Christ is heavenly bread, the food of the saints, as He said: "Unless you eat My flesh and drink My blood" (John 6:53). In the same way, the devil is the food of impure people who want nothing to do with the light, but want to do the works of darkness. Therefore, in order to turn His people away from vices, God commands them to feed on virtue, which is humbleness of mind, willingness to endure humiliation, and the acknowledgment of God.

Fasting like this not only makes God look on us favorably, but it also prepares us for the Easter Feast by setting our hearts on things above. Consider the facts written in the Scriptures about great men of old. Moses was fasting when he talked with God and received the Law. That very great and holy man Elijah, when fasting, was thought worthy of divine vision. At the end of his life he was taken up like the Lord, who ascended into heaven. Daniel, too, though a very young man, was entrusted with things no one else knew while he was fasting. He was made to understand the king's problems and was given divine visions. . . .

Therefore, brothers and sisters, let us nourish our souls with divine food, Jesus Christ the Word. And,

fasting with both body and soul as God desires, let us
keep this great and saving fast as we should.

It should be apparent, then, that the proper attitude
while fasting is crucial if it is to be of any benefit to us.
Mere abstinence from types of food, or even from all
food, is not in itself enough to provide a spiritual benefit.
An inner fast of the heart must accompany the outward
fast. Otherwise fasting may be detrimental rather than
helpful, producing a spirit of legalism or of arrogance.
Saint John Chrysostom offers us an exhortation on the
nature of true fasting:

> Do you fast? Give me proof by what you do! What do I
> mean? Well, if you see a poor man, take pity on him! If
> you see a beautiful woman, don't dwell on fornication!
> Don't fast by the mouth, but also by the eye, the ear, the
> feet, the hands—all members of your body. Let your
> hands fast by being pure from stealing and taking things
> others should have. Let your feet fast by not running
> to watch things you should not. Let your eyes fast,
> being taught not to look at things they should not, and
> especially not to stare at beautiful women. . . . Let the
> ear fast also. The fasting of the ear consists in refusing to
> listen to evil talk and rumors. . . . Let the mouth, too, fast
> from disgraceful talk.

Thus, fasting is not carried out for its own sake. We
fast in order to pray. Further, these two should be joined

by works of love and compassion, that is, almsgiving. With these three joined to a proper spirit of devotion, one is better able to prepare himself to celebrate the joy of our resurrection life in Christ.

Especially in the specified seasonal fastings of the Church, not only is the observance of fasting with the stomach, eyes, ears, feet, and hands important, but also the outward rules for fasting. The categories of foods from which the individual abstains are not simply a matter of personal choice. In other words, the Church in her wisdom has outlined not only the days and seasons of fasting, but also the levels of fasting to be observed during those times. When everyone enters into fasting in accordance with the guidelines laid down by his or her spiritual father, spiritual health prevails and Church unity is maintained.

Fasting: An Overview

Let's take a short look at what fasting is and is not, why we do it, how to do it and when.

1) First, what is meant by fasting as seen by the Church?

• Fasting is voluntary abstinence from food or drink for spiritual reasons, although it also tends to benefit health.

• Fasting may involve complete avoidance of food and/or drink for part of a day or a longer period of time.

• Fasting may simply be cutting down on the amount of food, which is done in all types of fasting; or it may include elimination of some categories of food on certain days of the week, or for a season such as Lent.

• But (as we have noted) not only food and drink are to be abstained from. There are many other things, some of them of positive value in moderation: material pleasures such as entertainment through reading or the arts; daydreaming, fantasies, and lustful thoughts, all of which the Church Fathers considered sinful; idle talk, gossip; looking at things one shouldn't; and going places one ought to avoid.

2) However, just because people sometimes have misconceptions about fasting, let us also ask what it is not.

• In the practice of the Church, fasting is not a law we keep to be a valid member of the Church or to gain the favor of God.

• The fasting practice of the Church is not a blanket rule imposed to the same degree on everybody despite circumstances of health, age, spiritual maturity, or heart's desire. Although the Lord expected His disciples to fast, He gave them no commandment to do so.

• Fasting is not an end in itself; it is always done for other reasons: prayer, self-control, and humility in particular.

3) The Church Fathers say gluttony, although not the worst of sins, is the one most often leading to all the other vices.

• Saint John Climacus, for example, says it opens the door to fornication and pride, especially, as well as to drowsiness.

• As long as one is a little hungry, he is not so

likely to be drawn by sexual lust, but when the belly is full, he is more inclined to seek the further gratification of sex.

• With a full stomach one is also the more subject to the most deadly vice of all: pride, described by the Fathers writing in the *Philokalia* as the one vice that, instead of destroying only one or two virtues, as the other sins do, annihilates the whole lot of them.

We see, therefore, that by keeping a tight grip on our appetite for food and drink, both by moderation at all times and by periods of fasting, we avoid much evil and clear away obstacles to knowing the holy God and to receiving eternal life.

4) Along with aiding self-control, the chief reason for fasting, as going beyond moderation alone, is to help us to pray more consistently and intensely, hence more effectively. We have already seen that fasting for its own sake can do more harm than good—even leading to spiritual pride, the vice of Satan himself, and the worst of all evils. Only a small fraction of people in the Church keep the weekly and seasonal fasts in their full strictness, but each is encouraged to do only what he has heart, ability, and circumstances to accomplish. The purpose of fasting is not to prove how strong we are, but, if anything, the opposite. We fast to fill our heart and mind with prayer, which cannot be done if we are sated and drowsy with food.

5) Together with self-control and effective prayer, a major goal of fasting is humility. As we submit to it under the leadership of God's Holy Spirit, we are

reminded of how weak we are. As fasting helps to destroy or prevent pride, it fosters the opposite of this vice: humility. It brings us to our senses to see and keep in mind how limited and mortal we are. Even our attempt to carry out a true fast dispels fantasies about our abilities and strengths—both physical and spiritual. We are reminded of how dependent on God we are.

6) We are to keep in mind, however, that as Christians our major concern, far outweighing bodily health or having a few more years in this fleeting present world, is to be prepared for eternal life with God. This, then, is the main reason for fasting, self-control, or any other virtuous action.

GIVING: TITHES, ALMS, AND PRAYER

Our Lord said, "Where your treasure is, there your heart will be also" (Matthew 6:21). Contrary to what many people think, one does not necessarily put one's treasure where one's heart is, but the heart follows the treasure.

The Old Testament gives us a pattern for worship and service to God. One important part of this, a very basic aspect of worship itself, is the giving of a portion of our material goods. A convenient baseline or minimum for this was the tithe—one tenth of one's gross income from all sources. A tithe was just the rock bottom for a faithful Israelite to give (and there was more than one "tithe"). In addition, the people of Israel were encouraged to give additional gifts and offerings for the service of God and the poor. God took (and takes!) this matter of offerings quite seriously, as Malachi says:

"Will a man rob God?
Yet you have robbed Me!
But you say,
'In what way have we robbed You?'
In tithes and offerings.
You are cursed . . .
Even this whole nation.
Bring all the tithes into the storehouse,
That there may be food in My house,
And try Me now in this,"
Says the Lord of hosts,
"If I will not open for you the windows of heaven
And pour out for you such blessing
That there will not be room enough to receive it.

"And I will rebuke the devourer for your sakes,
So that he will not destroy the fruit of your ground . . .
And all nations will call you blessed
For you will be a delightful land . . ." (Malachi 3:8–12).

It is no small thing that, as God says through Malachi, if one does not tithe and give, one loses that much and more to the "devourer"—forfeiting God's protection from this loss. Today, if we want to be part of a Church that is truly filled with God's presence and delightful, drawing many people into it and towards eternal life, we are wise to put our money where our mouth is.

One thousand years before Malachi, Moses included tithing in his Law:

> You shall truly tithe all the increase of your grain that the
> field produces year by year. And you shall eat before the
> Lord your God, in the place where He chooses to make
> His name abide, the tithe of your grain and your new
> wine and your oil, of the firstborn of your herds and
> your flocks, that you may learn to fear the Lord your
> God always. But if the journey is too long for you, so
> that you are not able to carry the tithe . . . then you shall
> exchange it for money . . . and go to the place which the
> Lord your God chooses (Deuteronomy 14:22–25).

Someone might observe that we are not under the
Jewish Law, but under grace—why then should we be
encouraged to tithe? It is true that we are not subject to
giving any particular minimum to be in the Church or
God's Kingdom. What God really wants is us, not our
money.

Before we leave the idea behind as unworthy,
however, let us note that tithing did not begin with
Moses and his Law. Centuries earlier, Abraham, who
is the spiritual father of us in the Church as well as the
ancestor of the Hebrews, paid tithes to Melchizedek, a
type of Christ as High Priest: "Then Melchizedek king of
Salem brought out bread and wine; he was the priest of
God Most High. And he blessed him. . . . And [Abraham]
gave him a tithe of all" (Genesis 14:18–20).

In the Book of Hebrews we read of this passage:

> Now consider how great this man was, to whom even
> the patriarch Abraham gave a tenth of the spoils. And

indeed those who are of the sons of Levi, who receive
the priesthood, have a commandment to receive tithes;
from the people according to the law, that is, from
their brethren, though they have come from the loins
of Abraham; but he whose genealogy is not derived
from them received tithes from Abraham and blessed
him who had the promises . . . Here mortal men
receive tithes, but there he receives them, of whom it is
witnessed that he lives. Even Levi, who receives tithes,
paid tithes through Abraham, so to speak, for he was
still in the loins of his father when Melchizedek met him
(Hebrews 7:4–10).

Regular giving of financial or other material goods
has always been a practice of God's people—a spiritual
practice. During the history of the Church, there have
been periods of time in many countries when the Church
was supported by the state rather than by direct giving
of the people. But where do you suppose the state got
its money? From the people, in one way or another! God
grant that we give voluntarily, as unto the Lord.

Some countries have separation of Church and state,
which they feel is good because of the religious freedom
allowed, and because the state cannot manipulate the
Church by holding the purse strings. But that means
Christians living there must support the Church directly
with their tithes and offerings. If they do not, they are
worse than unbelievers.

If money seems unspiritual and unworthy of any
connection with God and worship, we must remember

that God became incarnate for us: this means He took on not only our human flesh, but matter itself, drawing the whole universe to redemption. Thus, even something as "worldly" as money and our use of it is crucial to our life in the Church, which is the beginning of God's New Creation and Eternal Kingdom.

In speaking against greed and anxiety, our Lord Jesus Christ told His hearers, "Sell what you have and give alms; provide yourselves money bags which do not grow old, a treasure in the heavens that does not fail, where no thief approaches nor moth destroys. For where your treasure is, there your heart will be also" (Luke 12:33, 34). Those are wise words for us to hear. If our hearts are centered upon the Kingdom of God, devoted to Him, we will be willing to give generously from all that we have—and we will be better able to pray freely. If, then, we would be friends and servants of Christ our God, let us remember the poor.

In summary, let us take note: fasting, almsgiving, and prayer are all physical acts demonstrating our love for, and obedience to, God. We are created in the image and likeness of God and to worship God. Doing His will—the will of our one Master—is one aspect of this worship, manifested through our fasting, giving of alms, and prayer out of love for Him.

Fasting is a means of controlling our physical desires and our thought life—rejecting pride and worldly concerns in order to reorient ourselves to God. Further, if we will let it, fasting—accompanied by a growing attention to spiritual concerns—allows us to concentrate more effectively on our prayers. It goes without saying, therefore, that we should orient ourselves to accompany fasting with increased sorrow for our sins. We do not fast as a law, but to strengthen ourselves and to build humility.

Almsgiving is also a physical demonstration of our love for God and neighbor—for our heart will follow our desire and our actions (and vice versa). Knowing and loving God requires active participation and constant attention to His will—a living of that will. All we obtain and possess comes by the grace of God, and we are to share this abundant grace with those in need. Never must we forget the words of the Apostle James, "faith without works is dead"—and one way we demonstrate our faith is by the work of giving alms. We have been called to imitate Christ, and giving of what we have (actually, of what we have been given) is a reflection of His gift of Himself for us. When we show mercy and compassion, gratitude and humility, by such acts as giving alms, His life shines forth.

Prayer is the primary work of our life. All of life is to be lived worshiping God, and the more our heart is enriched through prayer, the stronger our feelings toward God grow. Through praying without ceasing, we join ourselves to God, making ourselves available to be filled with the glory of God. In addition, our personal prayers orient and prepare us to join in the corporate prayers of the Church, assisting us to participate more fully in the common worship. We wish to enter into the sacraments with pure hearts, so we pray for God's will to be worked out in us.

These three, then—fasting, almsgiving, and prayer—are both physical and spiritual means of drawing and binding us to God, demonstrating our love for Him. We do not forget Saint Paul's words, "Now abide faith, hope, love, these three; but the greatest of these is love" (1 Corinthians 13:13). Fasting, almsgiving, and prayer are all direct outcomes and demonstrations of our love for God.

STUDY QUESTIONS

1. *What connection have you found for yourself between fasting and prayer?*
2. *What experience have you had of the relationship between giving and prayer?*

CHAPTER 6

Personal and Corporate Prayer

Our Lord, in two passages found in the Gospel of Matthew, gives us specific instructions about prayer—instructions which might seem contradictory:

1) In the Sermon on the Mount: "And when you pray, you shall not be like the hypocrites. For they love to pray standing in the synagogues and on the corners of the streets, that they may be seen by men. Assuredly, I say to you, they have their reward. But you, when you pray, go into your room, and when you have shut your door, pray to your Father who is in the secret place; and your Father who sees in secret will reward you openly" (Matthew 6:5, 6).

2) Then, later, to His disciples: "Again I say to you that if two of you agree on earth concerning anything that they ask, it will be done for them by My Father in heaven. For where two or three are gathered together in My name, I am there in the midst of them" (Matthew 18:19, 20).

The first passage refers to how we pray when we, individually, go before the Lord. The second has to do with corporate prayer—when we join with others in agreement about something. We must ask the question: Are these instructions contradictory? Or do they, instead, fit together?

PRAYING TOGETHER AND PRAYING ALONE

We shall see that not only are these instructions consistent with each other, but also we can only follow them properly if we remember and obey both:

1) We do have to learn to pray alone (though in a larger sense we are never alone, for Father, Son, and Holy Spirit, along with all the hosts of heaven, are always present when we truly pray). We must bring all our needs and all our sins to God in intimate and personal prayer.

2) And we must also join with others in common and joint prayer. In a true and paradoxical sense, our ability to do each depends upon our practice of the other.

Nobody is a Christian all by himself. We are members of the Body of Christ (Romans 12:4, 5; 1 Corinthians 10:16, 17; 12:12–27; Ephesians 1:22, 23; 4:4–16; Colossians 1:18). Further, it is as members of that Body, the Church, that we pray—even when we are alone. As members of the Church, we pray together in the services and learn our devotional practices and our rule of prayer— that is, the habitual form and order of prayer we practice.

Consequently, corporate prayer and individual prayer are more than complementary. They are, in fact, directly joined together as inseparable aspects of our devotional life. Neither is complete without the other—and either may even be dangerous to our spiritual health if practiced in isolation. Solitary prayer can degenerate into an individualistic pietism, without substance or foundation. And when people who have no training in the prayer forms of the Church, as they have been established through the centuries, try to join with others in worship, they find it difficult to practice true community prayer. Too often the result is a sort of crowd prayer, that of an incoherent multitude, rather than true community prayer. Or it becomes a mere formality and performance.

Preparing for Corporate Prayer

For that very reason, the Church expects her people to prepare themselves through personal prayer in their rooms at home, and then come together to pray the prayers formed through the ages into the worship and prayer services.

What then shall we say? That we begin to pray at home and then go to Church? Or that we pray together at Church and then go home to pray in our rooms? Neither question is quite the right one. The matter is far more complex and reaches into:

- the way in which we were reared;
- how we came into contact with and began to use individual prayers;
- how and when we came into contact with the services of the Church and began to participate in them;
- the attitudes sown in our hearts by our parents, our associates, and our culture;
- what we have learned about knowing God, knowing His people, communing with them, and communing with Him;

- the guidance of our spiritual father (guide);
- and certainly how we are now responding to all of the above.

"Private Devotions"

As we proceed, then, let us remember these things, for we must work through them as we continue, throughout our lives, to learn about prayer. As we implied above, the term "private devotions," so commonly used among Christians today, is a misleading expression. To some it carries the implication that prayer is a private matter to be practiced according to an individual's inclination. In fact, however, prayer practiced in our rooms, apart from others, is (among other things) an obligatory preparation for our meeting together to offer our common prayer with, as it were, a single heart and mouth.

Our personal prayers or devotions must follow a definite form or design, with little room for improvisation—especially at first. That is why we need a "rule of prayer." For even alone in our room, we must not pray for ourselves alone. We are, as noted above, never alone on our knees (or standing or falling prostrate on our face) before the Father. For the Father is not just the Father of the lone individual, but the Father of us all.

We Never Pray Alone

When we are praying, we are to be aware that many others are also doing the same thing before the same heavenly Father—with whom are not only the Son and the Holy Spirit, but the saints and angels as well. And each of us must bring to God not only our own needs and those of our family, but the needs, requests, and sorrows of the whole world.

Our personal prayer should, in fact, steadily become catholic—inclusive and universal. Through our union with our brothers and sisters in the Church, our praying heart is meant to become enlarged to embrace all the needs and sorrows of the whole of humanity—even though we know the specifics of only a very few. This spirit enables individual people to join together as brothers and sisters and for us to agree concerning what we are to ask from the Lord.

We Must Pray Together

Then, from the other direction, corporate prayer is also a personal obligation. Each of us who is a member of the Body of Christ is obligated to join in the common life of that Body, and especially in the common prayer and worship. This corporate character of all Christian worship and prayer has been a constant emphasis in the Church from its earliest days—as evidenced by Saint Cyprian of Carthage (martyred September 14, 258) in his commentary on the Lord's Prayer:

> Above all, the Teacher of Peace and Master of Unity did not want prayer to be viewed as something individual- istic and self-centered. Accordingly, when we pray, we must not think only of ourselves. . . . For us, prayer is public and communal; and when we pray, we do so, not

for one, but for the whole People, because we, the whole People, are one.

Saint Cyprian's commentary, by the way, is one we should read and reread, for it has been that study of the Lord's Prayer most cherished through the centuries. When Saint Hilary of Poitiers (d. c. 367) wrote his commentary on the Gospel of Saint Matthew a hundred years later, he did not comment on this prayer, for, he said, "Saint Cyprian has said it all." Let us review this most important prayer briefly from Saint Cyprian's perspective.

LORD, TEACH US TO PRAY

Of all the many prayers to be found in the Old and New Testaments, this one is given directly from the Lord—in response to a request from His disciples: "Lord, teach us to pray" (Luke 11:1). His response was, "When you pray, say . . ." And there followed the words we know as "The Lord's Prayer" or "The Our Father." Consequently, this prayer has been on the lips of Christians more than any other, and devout Orthodox Christians pray it several times a day.

Our Father Who Art in Heaven

In the version of the Lord's Prayer given in Matthew, in the midst of the Sermon on the Mount, our Lord begins with the words, "Our Father who art in heaven." A short time before He had said, "Blessed are those who hunger and thirst for righteousness, for they shall be filled" (Matthew 5:6). When we set out upon the path of salvation, seeking God with as much zeal as we can muster, that hunger will begin to be there—as it was in the disciples. By prayer, and especially this prayer, we strengthen that hunger. As he begins to comment on the prayer, Saint Cyprian writes:

> The precepts of the gospel, dear friends, are truly lessons from God: foundations upon which to build our hope, pillars of support to strengthen our faith, food to cheer our heart, guiding rudders in life, aids to our salvation, which, by instructing the receptive minds of believers, lead us to the kingdom of heaven.

The very invocation, "our Father," is a constant reminder of our standing before God—that we have been raised up from the status of enemies to that of children, given by grace that which we do not have by nature. I do not know if there is any way we can go beyond a mere beginning of understanding of the meaning of this. Most especially, we should never forget the marvel of what we are privileged to do—to address the heavenly God as "Father." For, as the Apostle John wrote, "He came to His own, and His own did not receive Him. But as many as received Him, to them He gave the right to become children of God, to those who believe in His Name" (John 1:12).

The only proper way for us to live, then, is as true temples of God (1 Corinthians 3:16). Our way of life is not to be incompatible with the presence of the Holy Spirit—we are to become progressively more spiritually minded, thinking and doing only what is good and proper. Ages ago, God said, "Those who honor Me I will honor, and those who despise Me shall be lightly esteemed" (1 Samuel 2:30). Saint Paul also had something to say on this matter, writing, "You are not your own. . . . for you were bought at a price; therefore glorify God in your body and in your spirit, which are God's" (1 Corinthians 6:19, 20).

Nor should we neglect the small word "our," for by this word our Lord made it clear He did not want us to pray as isolated individuals, centered only upon ourselves. He wished us to keep the whole body of His people in mind, each praying not for himself, but for all. That is a vital lesson for us to learn in a world which teaches us to reach for our own goal, to look out for ourselves, for it runs counter to our selfishness—which is exalted and fed by all the messages of popular culture. Quite obviously, His disciples learned this lesson, for we read that after His Ascension, they "all continued with one accord in prayer and supplication, with the women and Mary the mother of Jesus, and with His brothers" (Acts 1:14).

That our Father is "in heaven" should not throw us off track, for we already know God does not dwell in a physical form at some place on earth or far out in space. He is truly omnipresent, truly everywhere, yet not to be pinned down anywhere by our physical senses. Heaven indicates His superiority to any place, yet His availability to us at all times and everywhere. When we pray, then, we are to expect He hears. He is indeed, as Christ Jesus our Lord said, within us: "The Kingdom of God is within you" (Luke 17:21).

Hallowed Be Thy Name

Our Lord tells us to pray, "hallowed be Thy Name," but it is clearly absurd for us to pray that any more holiness be added to the all-holy God—He who is perfect and the Giver of holiness. Consequently, we are forced to one more humbling conclusion: that our prayer is for His Name to be hallowed in us. We plead that we who have once been sanctified in baptism may continue in that which has been begun, growing in grace and knowledge of Him. Only then will His Name be hallowed in us. Nor should we ever allow ourselves to forget how short we fall in fully and properly doing so. Saint Paul reminds us what we were and at the same time, what we are in Christ:

> Do you not know that the unrighteous will not inherit the kingdom of God? Do not be deceived. Neither fornicators, nor idolaters, nor adulterers, nor homosexuals, nor sodomites, nor thieves, nor covetous, nor drunkards, nor revilers, nor extortioners will inherit the kingdom of God. And such were some of you. But you were washed, but you were sanctified, but you were justified in the name of the Lord Jesus and by the Spirit of our God (1 Corinthians 6:9–11).

This is truly something to pray for, and to work for, urgently every day of our lives: that the sanctification and new life we received from God be preserved in us.

Thy Kingdom Come

By our Lord's direction, we continue by praying, "Thy Kingdom come." People whose hearts are set on wealth go after it by every possible means—there is literally nothing they will stop at. That pursuit, however, is doomed to an unhappy conclusion. In the end they have lost all, for as the Savior said, "What profit is it to a man if he gains the whole world and loses his own soul?" Now, what are we to do, who desire the salvation which comes from God?

We cry, "Thy Kingdom come!" that we, His people, may experience His Kingdom, just as we asked that His Name be made holy in us. Certainly, there is no time when God did not reign—in fact, there is no beginning of His reign, which is eternal. What we look for in His command to pray, "Thy Kingdom come," is His intent for His people. For one thing, we look for the coming again of Christ our Lord—not as He came in His first advent, in humility, but in His true glory as God. Saint Paul writes that He "alone has immortality, dwelling in unapproachable light" (1 Timothy 6:16), so we look for the majesty of His coming—"in," as He said, "the glory of His Father with His angels" (Matthew 16:27).

This truth and this prayer alone should cause us to pay attention to how we live—not carelessly, not in sin, not distracted into laziness and love of pleasure, but in a manner suitable to those who are called to holiness and God's will. For if we hope to reign with Him, we must also suffer with Him, enduring to the end (2 Timothy 2:12). If we have renounced the world and all its wealth and honors to dedicate ourselves to Christ, then our lives must also be dedicated to His Kingdom, now and forever. The haunting words of His prophecy should also echo in our spirit: "Many will come from east and west, and sit down with Abraham, Isaac, and Jacob in the kingdom of heaven. But the sons of the kingdom will be cast out into outer darkness. There will be weeping and gnashing of teeth" (Matthew 8:11, 12).

Thy Will Be Done

He continues, telling His disciples to pray, "Thy will be done on earth as it is in heaven." Those words are certainly not a prayer for God to do what He wants done, but that we be enabled to do what He wants us to do. David, the prophet and psalmist, wrote, "Show me Your ways, O LORD; teach me Your paths. Lead me in Your truth and teach me, for You are the God of my salvation" (Psalm 25:4, 5). All who are in Christ by faith are taught by God, and we are among them—if we will. But the devil would have us disobey God in thought and deed, and our own sinful passions agree; so we fervently pray God's will be done in us. Indeed, we truly want all mankind to do His will, to live as they should, to know and practice what is good in His sight. And where does it begin, if not in us?

We know His will is done in heaven by all His host,

so we start there: "as it is in heaven." To do His will we need His help, His protection, His guidance, for none of us is adequate to do this on our own without His grace and mercy. Remembering that "our citizenship is in heaven" (Philippians 3:20), we must, therefore, "cleanse ourselves from all filthiness of the flesh and spirit, perfecting holiness in the fear of God" (2 Corinthians 7:1). Our Lord Himself said, "I have come down from heaven, not to do My own will, but the will of Him who sent Me" (John 6:38), and if that is what He did, should we do something else? Our prayer is that first we, then all, do His will as it is in heaven, living godly, holy, and blameless lives, free from all corruption—like the angels in heaven.

Give Us This Day Our Daily Bread

Then we pray, "Give us this day our daily bread"— sometimes rendered "our necessary" or "our needful" bread. We may take this petition in either a physical or a spiritual sense—or both—for both senses are applicable, since both are necessary. It is no less appropriate to pray for the simple bread our bodies need each day than to pray for that which came down from heaven and was given for the life of the world.

No matter how constant our times may be or seem, history teaches us that our lives may change suddenly, so we ask for our daily bread—not for excess or for wealth, but for the needs of the day alone. If it seems to be there without our prayer, let us not forget to pray, and if there is none, let us nevertheless pray. If we doubt, we become like those Israelites who murmured, saying, "Can God prepare a table in the wilderness?" (Psalm 78:19)—rather than like David, who sang, "You prepare a table before me in the presence of my enemies" (Psalm 23:5). Let us, therefore, "casting all [our] care upon Him" (1 Peter 5:7), ask Him for what we need and no more.

Taking the words in the spiritual sense, we know that all who live in Christ receive His Body as heavenly food. He told His disciples, "I am the living bread which came down from heaven. If anyone eats of this bread, he will live forever; and the bread that I shall give is My flesh, which I shall give for the life of the world" (John 6:51). Those who eat His bread, properly partaking of the Eucharist, have life. We ask for this necessary bread, praying that it not be taken from us.

Forgive Us Our Trespasses

"Forgive us our trespasses," we pray, "as we forgive those who trespass against us." When we pray those words from our heart, we acknowledge what we are— not thinking great things of ourselves, not considering ourselves strong, but weak. For we remember, there is no one who lives and does not sin. Who is there who can say he has an absolutely pure heart? Who is confident he is not defiled by sin? Even the Apostle Paul said, "I know of nothing against myself, yet I am not justified by this; but He who judges me is the Lord" (1 Corinthians 4:4). The path to salvation is paved with confession, the words of those who are willing to say to Him who purifies the wicked, "Forgive us our trespasses."

The Apostle John puts our condition very clearly in a few words: "If we say that we have no sin, we deceive ourselves, and the truth is not in us. If we confess our sins, He is faithful and just to forgive us our sins and to cleanse us from all unrighteousness" (1 John 1:8, 9). If we truly admit we have sinned, and seek this pardon from God, we first of all acknowledge He is to be feared—"Do not fear those who kill the body but cannot kill the soul. But rather fear Him who is able to destroy both soul and body in hell" (Matthew 10:28)—remembering His dread judgment seat. "For," as Saint Paul writes, "We must all appear before the judgment seat of Christ, that each one may receive the things done in the body, according to what he has done, whether good or bad" (2 Corinthians 5:10). At the same time, however, we also acknowledge the goodness and mercy of God in Christ, who is always ready to receive and to forgive the repentant sinner.

But there is still that second half to haunt us: "as we forgive those who trespass against us." If we are to ask forgiveness of God, we cannot be holding the sin of others against them. We are not the lords of others and cannot therefore grant them forgiveness of their sins against God and others. We can and must, however, forgive them to the extent they have sinned against us. Taking on this characteristic is essential for one who wishes to live a life conformed to God. Harboring resentment is incalculably damaging to us—physically, mentally, and spiritually. If we keep a sharp eye out for people to wrong us, holding slights, insults, and injuries in our hearts, we will have no place within for the love of God.

It is impossible to say how difficult it is for us to forget injuries (real or imagined) to us by others and to recover from the habit of building up resentment. Such inner activities build up their own energy within us and rob us of energies needed for prayer and for good, while doing such great damage. Nevertheless, we must give ourselves wholeheartedly to defeating such attitudes within. We must not forget Saint Paul, who wrote, "Being reviled, we bless; being persecuted, we endure; being defamed, we entreat" (1 Corinthians 4:12, 13). The example is first set by our Lord Himself, who, as Saint Peter writes, "when He was reviled, did not revile in return; when He suffered, He did not threaten, but committed Himself to Him who judges righteously" (1 Peter 2:23).

Lead Us Not into Temptation

This greatest of all prayers concludes with a brief phrase summing up all our petitions: simply, "and lead us not into temptation." This covers all possible harm the enemy can throw at us in this world—and from which we have certain and powerful protection if God delivers us and grants His aid, as we beseech. Saint Cyprian writes, "Once we have sought and obtained God's protection from evil, we stand safe and secure against all the machinations of the devil and the world."

STUDY QUESTIONS

1. *How are personal and corporate prayer associated in your experience?*
2. *How does the interrelationship of the two affect the manner and attitude with which you approach your rule of prayer?*
3. *What do the words of Saint Cyprian as quoted in this chapter have to do with the above?*
4. *Choose one of the petitions of the Lord's Prayer which especially strikes home to you just now and write down how it applies to you today—this very day.*
5. *What do you believe there is about forgiving others that is so difficult for us?*

CHAPTER 7

The Holy Sacrament of the Eucharist

Since we are not alone before God, but members of the Body of Christ, personal prayer is vitally connected with the mystery of the Church, a mystery visibly revealed in the corporate and sacramental worship of the Church. And the center of this corporate worship is the Eucharist—the sacrament, the Holy Mystery, established for us by our Lord at His Last Supper with His disciples (Matthew 26:26–28). In the Eucharist we find a double mystery—the Mystery of the Head and the Body, of the Lord and His people, the Church. And this mystery, the Eucharist, is a true revelation of the Son of God, of His redeeming work in and through His Incarnation.

ESSENTIAL QUALITIES OF THE EUCHARIST
We already know about four important weapons for fighting the unseen warfare:
- refusal to rely upon ourselves;
- unshakable hope in God;
- resisting and struggling with sin;
- prayer.

Now we come to another powerful weapon in this warfare: the most holy sacrament of the Eucharist. This sacrament is the highest of all sacraments and the most powerful and effective of all spiritual weapons. The four weapons of which we have spoken receive their power from the energies and gifts of grace obtained for us by the Blood of Christ. But the Eucharist is (in a true and heavenly mystery) the Body and Blood of Christ Himself—in which He is Himself present as God. When we use those first four weapons, we fight the enemy with His power.

Through the Eucharist our Lord Himself strikes down our enemy through us—or, rather, in union with us. For when we eat His Body and drink His Blood, we abide in Him and He in us—as He said: "He who eats My flesh and drinks My blood abides in Me, and I in him" (John 6:56). Therefore, when we overcome the enemies, it is the Blood of Christ which overcomes, as the Apostle John writes in Revelation: "And they overcame him [the devil] by the blood of the Lamb" (Revelation 12:11).

This most holy sacrament, this all-conquering weapon—or rather Christ present in it—can be actively received in a twofold manner: first, sacramentally, in the sacrament of Christ's Flesh and Blood, with the necessary preparation of our heart; second, inwardly and spiritually, in spirit and heart.

The first may take place as often as outer circumstances allow. The second can take place every moment—at all times. Thus, we may always have this all-powerful weapon in our hand, constantly wielding it against our enemies.

Pay attention to this, therefore, and partake of the Holy Mysteries of Christ as often as possible. But also endeavor to partake continually of Christ our Lord inwardly and spiritually. Our previous chapters on prayer give guidance on how we can do this.

The Mystery of the Eucharist

In the process of leading us in a mystical ascent to heaven during the Sundays and feastdays throughout the year, the Eucharist carries us through the whole of the incarnate life of our Lord, from Bethlehem to the Mount of Olives and Calvary, from His Resurrection to His Ascension, and on to our anticipation of His second and glorious Coming. And this experience is not merely a remembrance, but truly a re-presentation, a making-present-again in truth.

But let us remember—the two ways of the mystery of our prayer must be a whole. The Eucharist is the peak of Christian experience, the new fellowship of the redeemed community, the Church, in her Redeemer— and the greatest witness to the fullness of our union with Him and with each other. In that latter sense, whenever the Mystery of the Eucharist is celebrated, the Body of Christ—His Church—bears witness to her Lord and Master.

But there is far more to the Eucharist than a human witness. For there is indeed something to "come and see," as Jesus said (John 1:39). If we come with open heart and right faith, we can see and touch the Lord Himself, who is always present in His blessed Mysteries—present and truly visible to those who look with spiritual eyes. The teaching concerning His Body and

Blood must not be regarded as a mere theological theory or interpretation, nor as a kind of transformation in a material sense apparent to our five outer senses. It is, rather, a mystical fact attested to by sight—spiritual sight.

Nor is this presence of the Lord confined to the bread and wine, which does indeed become His Body and Blood. Christ is personally present, as the sovereign and only minister of the sacrament, as the true and eternal High Priest of the New Covenant. For the Eucharist is not simply something we do or offer. It is foremost what God is doing to us.

Celebration in Heaven

In that Eucharist, we celebrate in heaven, where Christ is once again with His faithful as in the Last Supper—for every celebration of the Eucharist is that Last Supper itself, extended and continued. This identity is stressed throughout the whole of the Liturgy in the Orthodox Church.

The Eucharist is not a repetition or "re-enactment"—for no repetition of the Last Supper or of Calvary is possible. The Eucharist is one, that one Lord's Supper, but it is revealed again and again, as it is celebrated in the Church. For the sacrifice of Christ was universal and all-inclusive—it occurred once, for every one, for everything, and for all time. The depth of meaning in our Communion is to be found in the truth that at every celebration, we are taken back to the Upper Room at the moment of the Last Supper itself, when and where the sacrament was first instituted and administered by the Savior Himself—and at the same time to the heavenlies and the presence of the saints and angels.

The Mystery is one and always the same, just as the sacrifice is one and the Table is always the same. There is not one Lamb slain yesterday and another today, one slain here and another there. No, there is now, always, and everywhere the one, very same Lamb of God, "who takes away the sin of the world" (John 1:29)—that is, the Lord Jesus Christ Himself. Christ is present both as the Priest and the Victim, both celebrating the sacrament Himself, and giving His precious Body and Blood to His members as the food of redemption, as the food of the life eternal.

The Church simply receives the gift. Yet she is not passive, even while receiving the gift of the redemption. In the sacrament Christ is not separated from His Body, the Body which is His Church. The mystery of the Church lies in the fact that Christ abides in the faithful. And they, by faith, abide in Him.

In the world the Church endures and persists, carrying on the ministry of redemption. Yet we may even more truly say that it is Christ who continues His ministry in and through the Church. We are called upon to follow Him—to walk in His steps (1 Peter 2:21). Nor is this simply a commandment to do what He did. It is rather a command implying an existential and mystical identification of us with Him, of the members of the Body with the Head.

The Unity of the Body of Christ and Heavenly Food

Thus, the Eucharist, being the mystery of the Church, is in a sense the realization of the Church. For the Church takes her reality from the fact that she is gathered in her Lord, to be His Body. And that reality is expressed in that her members are incorporated into Him and His resurrected life—and are nourished on the same spiritual food and filled by the Spirit with that very same resurrected life. The unity of the Church is the unity of the Spirit (Ephesians 4:3) and the unity of faith (Ephesians 4:13), whereby she and her members partake of the grace of the mystery. We are one Body because we partake of the same Bread of Life, the same heavenly food.

Consequently, the Church can be said in a certain sense to be the "growing fullness" of Christ. That is, she, as His Body, grows through the sacraments. That means her unity is a gift of God, not a human accomplishment. Nevertheless, it includes and implies human participation as well—an active response, the cooperation of the redeemed with their Savior.

Common Worship

The Liturgy of the Eucharist is truly an act of common worship—made up by the common agreement of many to gather and pray together. That, of course, distinguishes it from, yet connects it with our personal prayer. The very name "liturgy" is derived from a Greek word meaning literally, "the work of the people," suggesting in itself a common action. And the Liturgy is truly an action, not just a word.

In this connection, it is unsurprising, and indeed significant, that all eucharistic prayers are composed in the plural form—"we" and "us," not "I" and "me." And most especially, the prayer of consecration is said by the priest in the plural—for he is offering prayers in the name of and on behalf of the faithful, of all the people. The priest does not celebrate in his own name, but in the name of all the people, for the gifts are offered by the people and set forth on the altar for consecration on their behalf.

As we know, it is only the priest who is given authority to offer the common prayers and to speak in the name of all. And his authority to do so is not given by the people, but by Christ Himself, who is the true Minister of all mysteries. The priest does not represent only the congregation, but Christ above all. Indeed, as the priest stands at the altar, offering, it is Christ who stands offering. Christ is truly ministering to His people, through human mediation. Authority is given to the priest not *by* the congregation, but *for* the congregation, as one of the many and diverse gifts of the Holy Spirit.

We Pray

When the priest says, in the name of the whole Church, "We pray . . .," the "we" has a double meaning. It signifies the unity of the assembled Church, the undivided Christian fellowship of all those who pray: "You, who have given us the grace to pray together . . ."

And this praying together is not a mere composite of many separate, private prayers. The true unity of prayer presupposes a mutual identification of those who join and agree in that prayer. Thus, we pray not as isolated individuals, but truly as members of the mystical Body of Christ (cf. 1 Corinthians 12:27; Ephesians 4:12).

Our Common Love

In the Liturgy of Saint John Chrysostom the prayer of consecration is preceded by a solemn invitation: "Let us love one another, that with one accord we may confess the Father, Son, and Holy Spirit, blessed Trinity, one in essence and undivided."

Through love in Christ we may have one accord, one mind—to be spiritually bonded. Saint Paul puts it this way: "with all lowliness and gentleness, with longsuffering, bearing with one another in love, endeavoring to keep the unity of the Spirit in the bond of peace" (Ephesians 4:2, 3)—"but above all these things put on love, which is the bond of perfection" (Colossians 3:14). This bond recalls to us that we are united to Christ in baptism, for "as many of us as were baptized into Christ Jesus were baptized into His death. Therefore we were buried with Him through baptism into death, that just as Christ was raised from the dead by the glory of the Father, even so we also should walk in newness of life. For if we have been united together in the likeness of His death, certainly we also shall be in the likeness of His resurrection" (Romans 6:3–5). And it is only in this bonding, this union, of our hearts and minds that we can approach and acknowledge the ultimate mystery of the Divine Unity: Three Persons, One God.

Our Unity in Christ
The mystery of the Holy Trinity is the mystery of a perfect unity of many: of the Three who are One. And this mystery is to be reflected on the human level. The Church, as a union, a joining of many, is the image on earth of the divine unity of the Holy Trinity. For the Church, established by Christ, is the new form and mode of human life, a true joining in one Body, not a mere association of individuals. And in its essence it is a true contrast to and contradiction of the idea of selfish individualism.

Thus, love makes the difference. Only love, in Christ, can enable human persons to bring their offerings to God in a true and worthy fashion. It is not simply because the lack of peace and love would be a personal failure, but just because we, the whole people of God, should be one, that, in the words of Saint Cyprian of Carthage, "When we pray, we do so, not for one, but for the whole people, because we, the whole people, are one" (On the Lord's Prayer, 8).

The Whole Church
But that "we" in the Liturgy has another, and even deeper, meaning and connotation. It also points to the universal fullness and unity of the Church. Every eucharistic Liturgy is celebrated in communion with the whole Church, of every place and every time. It is, in

fact, in the name of that whole Church that the Liturgy is celebrated. Spiritually, the whole Church takes an invisible yet very real part every time the Liturgy is celebrated, as does the whole of the angelic host.

Thus, the unity of prayer transcends space, time, and realms. Just as it includes all generations and all ages, there is no division between the living and the departed within the Church, for the departed are not dead. The power of death has been overcome (Hebrews 2:14) and death itself has been abolished by the glorious Resurrection of our Lord, who is the Head of His Body. For as we joyfully sing on Easter morning, He has trampled down death by death, bestowing life on those in the tomb. With His Resurrection, there is no final separation between earth and heaven. And therein lies the new spiritual climate which is that of the Church, for in Christ the two are joined.

Death Has No Power over Us

Yes, it is true. In the unity of the Body of Christ, death loses its power to separate us. The departed, who rest in the peace of Christ, are still with the living, for in Christ we are all one. Consequently, the departed are commemorated in every Liturgy:

> We offer to You this spiritual worship for those who in faith have gone on before us to their rest: forefathers, fathers, patriarchs, prophets, apostles, preachers, evangelists, martyrs, confessors, ascetics, and every righteous spirit made perfect in faith . . . and for all Your

saints, through whose intercessions watch over us, O
God. And remember all who have fallen asleep in hope
of the resurrection to eternal life, and give them rest
where the light of Your countenance watches over them
(Liturgy of St. John Chrysostom).

And this commemoration is not just a remembrance,
in the sense of a reminder. Nor is it simply a witness
of our human sympathy, love, and relationships. It is,
rather, an insight into and an experience of the mystical
communion of the members of the Body of Christ, living
and departed—in Christ our Risen Lord. In this sense
the Eucharist is the mystery of the Church and of Christ
her Head.

The Mystery of Redemption

In the Eucharist, the Church and her people are called
upon to be aware of her ultimate unity in Christ, antici-
pating the final perfection of that unity in the age to
come. There is a sense in which the Eucharist expresses
our communion and fellowship together as the people
of God (1 Corinthians 10:16, 17), but it is above all an
expression of the divine mystery of redemption (cf.
1 Corinthians 11:26). For the Eucharist is primarily
a work of God. And it is a mystery of Christ, who
redeems and unites us all in His Body (cf. Luke 22:19,
20), transcending all boundaries of space and time, age
and race.

Every time the Eucharist is celebrated, we witness
to—indeed, live within—this perfect unity, established

by our Incarnate and Risen Lord. And in that service we pray together in the name of all humanity—of all those who have been called and have responded to the call. It is corporately as the Church, the Body of Christ, that we pray. The whole Church prays with us and in us.

The Fullness of Life

Consequently, all the fullness of life is commemorated in our eucharistic prayers. The fullness of human existence is offered and dedicated to God in Christ—the whole of God's Providence remembered and acknowledged with true and heartfelt thanksgiving. Thus, we pray:

> Remembering this saving commandment and all that has been done for us: the Cross, the tomb, the Resurrection on the third day, the Ascension into heaven, the sitting at the right hand, and the second and glorious Coming, we offer You Your own, from what is Your own, for everyone and for everything (Liturgy of St. John Chrysostom).

We see, then, that the prayer of consecration is framed by the story of salvation. In every eucharistic celebration we bear witness to the redeeming plan and purpose of God—tracing all the stages of its coming about, as recorded in the Gospels.

The Role of Commemorations

The commemorations which follow in the prayers have a cosmic scope, including the whole of creation:

> We also offer You this reasonable and spiritual offering for the whole world, for the Holy Catholic and Apostolic Church, for those who live a pure and holy life, for all civil authorities and armed forces. Grant them, O Lord, peaceful times, so that we may live a quiet and peaceful life in all godliness and holiness (Liturgy of St. John Chrysostom).

The mentioning of categories of people and the names of others is especially important, for the name is not just a label, but refers to the person himself. And when we especially mention the names of members of the Church, this is a recognition that each person has a particular place in the completeness of the one Body. We also ask God to go beyond the limitations of our memory: "And remember, O God, all those whom we have not remembered, through ignorance, forgetfulness, or the multitude of names, for You know the name and age of each, even from his mother's womb" (Liturgy of St. Basil).

The eucharistic commemoration also embraces all the complex circumstances of our life on earth: "Be all things to all people, for You know each one and his request, his household, and his need" (Liturgy of Saint Basil). For the whole Body prays for all.

Acknowledgment and Witness

We see, then, that the eucharistic prayer is both an acknowledgment and a witness. God has acted first, to redeem the fallen human race: "Out of nothing You brought us into being and when we had fallen, raised us up again, and You have not ceased doing everything until You brought us to heaven and graciously gave us Your future Kingdom" (Liturgy of St. John Chrysostom).

So within the Liturgy of the Eucharist there is a doctrinal witness, an acknowledgment of the grace of God. He is the center of our attention and our action throughout.

Within the segment quoted above there is the acknowledgment also that the story of redemption is not yet completed. Christians live in expectation, for the Kingdom is yet to come. Still, the Church herself is a token of this glorious consummation. And she ever prays for the fulfillment: "Just as this loaf previously was scattered on the mountains and when it was gathered together became a unity, so may Your Church be gathered together from the ends of the earth into Your Kingdom" (The Didache, 9:4).

THE OTHER SACRAMENTS

All the rest of the sacraments (Holy Mysteries) are related to the Eucharist. Originally, they were all performed within the framework of the eucharistic Liturgy. And all of them are devoted to God's care for the members of the Body of Christ, the Church. We see this especially emphasized in the undivided liturgy of baptism and chrismation. But, following the Scriptures, we see the marks in the other sacraments as well—for instance, when Saint Paul's words in Ephesians 5 are read in the liturgy of marriage, and marriage is recognized as related to the mystery of the Church (Ephesians 5:31, 32).

Confession and Repentance

We must take special note of the mystery of confession and repentance and its role in the devotional prayers of the Church. For there are two features of this mystery. On the one hand there is the continual spiritual guidance given by a spiritual father (or guide) to his spiritual children. On the other hand there is that special liturgy of confession, repentance, and absolution. This sacrament is not directly connected with the Eucharist, but we must presume that the members of the Body of Christ will always keep in touch with their spiritual father, repenting and confessing as appropriate. That is, after all, our responsibility to ourselves, to God, and to each other. Violations of the commandments of God and failure to walk in His way are detrimental in every way, and must be repented and confessed. A disorderly life and continued violations of the commandments without repentance and confession compromise our spiritual status—as well as staining the Church. Not only should we ourselves not live that way, but such should not be permitted to go unheeded in any parish.

In the liturgy of the mystery of repentance, both confession and absolution are important. Confession springs basically from our own self-examination, repentance, and contrition (or "change of mind"). Absolution is declared by the priest, not by his own authority, but by that of Christ. The one who comes repenting and confessing should be prepared inwardly for that absolution—lest he go away unhealed. For the sacrament of confession is not simply a declaration of forgiveness, but primarily a spiritual cure.

Prayer and the Scriptures

In connection with our personal prayer and our corporate prayer, we must not underestimate the role of the Scriptures. First of all, the various liturgies of the Church are basically the preaching of the Word—an insistent and assertive proclamation of the Good News. If we examine the shape (the form and outline) of the orders of the various services (Vespers, Compline, Hours, and Matins, in addition to baptism and chrismation, the Eucharist, confession, marriage, and the rest), we find they are scriptural through and through. Indeed, the order of the history of God's plan of salvation is woven through them. Most of the hymns are biblical in their inspiration and content, and readings from the Scriptures are incorporated into all the worship services. Nor should we neglect the homily, which is an integral part of corporate worship—especially at the Eucharist.

The redeeming works of God wrought for His people throughout the history of our race therefore form the core of the services. For the reality of the Church is rooted in those works and bound to her Head, who worked them for her. Further, the structure of worship is corporate in its inspiration, its intent, and its form. Our personal devotions, in addition to their role in maintaining our relationship with God, also prepare us to share in the fellowship of the whole community of believers, the Church.

Communion with God

Obviously, the ultimate aim of worship is to enable us to establish and to perpetuate an intimate communion with God in Christ Jesus our Lord—and in the community of His Church. Let us therefore wholeheartedly direct our attention to all that God has given to build us up:

- personal prayer,
- the sacramental Mysteries of the Church,
- the prayer services of the Church,
- the fellowship of the faithful,
- the keeping of the commandments of God,
- and good works in the service of God, humanity, and all creation.

STUDY QUESTIONS

1. *Why are we called upon to pray individually and personally? Why did Christ tell us to pray in secret?*
2. *What is the relationship between praying at home and joining in the corporate prayer of the Church?*
3. *What are some specific things the Eucharist has meant to you in your life with God?*
4. *How does the Eucharist relate to the first four weapons given for our spiritual warfare?*

CHAPTER 8

The Eucharist
in the Life of Prayer

PREPARING TO RECEIVE THE EUCHARIST

To achieve the aim with which we approach the Eucharist, we must prepare ourselves and maintain a proper frame of heart and mind—before, during, and after Communion. Before Communion we must purify ourselves of all the filth of sin. Sometimes (and in our hearts we will know when) we will need to partake first of the sacrament of repentance and confession—not superficially, but fully revealing our hearts to our spiritual father. And we must do whatever he tells us—combining such action with a firm resolve to serve only our Lord Jesus Christ with our whole heart, soul, mind, and strength, and to do only what is acceptable to Him.

In the sacrament our Lord gives us His flesh and His blood—and with it the whole of Himself, the full force of His Incarnation, and all that goes with it. Therefore, when we think how insignificant our gifts to Him truly are compared with His gift, let us at least resolve in our heart to be diligent in doing all we can to His glory. And even if we gain possession of the greatest gift ever offered to Him by earthly or heavenly intelligent beings, let us declare our readiness to offer it without hesitation to His Divine Majesty.

Beginning Our Preparation

When we are to partake of the Eucharist, we must begin our preparation the evening before (or even earlier), by meditating on how much our Savior, the Son of God and God, desires that we, by partaking of this sacrament, give Him a place in our heart. For our aim and His great intent is that He be united with us, help us drive all sinful passions from our heart, and overcome all our enemies. Then we will be able to overcome and destroy (through the power of the sacrament) the Lord's enemies and our own.

This desire of the Lord is so great and so intense, no created mind can fully grasp it in its perfection. Therefore, in order to move even a little toward this understanding, we must try to impress deeply in our mind these two thoughts:

1) First, what inexpressible joy it is for the all-merciful God to be in the most genuine communion with us—as Wisdom itself testifies: "And my delight was with the sons of men" (Proverbs 8:31).

2) And second, how very much God hates sin, both because it prevents His union with us (which is truly and mystically very desirable to Him), and because it is directly opposed to His divine perfection. Since His nature is infinitely blessed, pure light and indescribable beauty, He cannot but totally abhor sin—which is the greatest extreme of evil, darkness, corruption, abomination, and shame in our souls. God's abhorrence of sin is so great that, from the very beginning, all the acts of divine Providence for us—and all the commands

and directions of the Old and New Testaments—were directed toward exterminating sin and wiping out its traces. This is most of all true of the indescribably awesome suffering and death of our Lord and Savior Jesus Christ, Son of God and God. Some theologians and teachers have even said that if it were necessary, our Lord Jesus would be ready to take upon Himself endless other deaths to destroy the power of sin. In this we can begin to see how strongly the wrath of God pursues sin.

Having, through such thoughts and contemplations, refreshed our memory of the greatness of God's desire to enter our heart in order to achieve there a final victory over our enemies—who are His enemies as well—we cannot help feeling a fervent desire to receive Him into ourselves in order that He may actually do so. Inspired by courage, then, and filled with boldness by the sure hope that our Heavenly Commander, Jesus our Lord, can enter, we are in a position to challenge to a fight whatever passion troubles us most (and which we want to overcome). Challenging, then, that passion, we will be enabled to strike it down with hatred, contempt, and disgust—at the same time arousing in ourselves the prayerful desire for that virtue which is directly opposite to the passion we fight.

On the Morning of Communion

Then, in the morning, a little while before the Holy Communion, let us make a mental survey of all the times we were carried away, did wrong, or sinned—since the last time we partook of Communion. We do well to remember especially the blindness and foolhardiness with which all this was done, as though for us there were no God who judges and rewards, who has seen it all, and who has borne terrible tortures and a shameful death on the Cross to deliver us from such things.

We must bring to our realization the fact that we disdained all this every time we inclined toward sin and put our own shameful lusts above the will of our God and Savior. Indeed, the face of our soul should be covered with shame when we realize our recklessness and lack of gratitude.

Still, we must not let ourselves be overwhelmed by the inner distress caused by all this—and we must cast out any hopelessness. In His infinite longsuffering, the Lord sees our repentance and our desire to serve Him alone from now on. In His mercy He comes to us and into us, in order to overwhelm and drown in the greatness of His lovingkindness the greatness of our ingratitude, our recklessness and lack of faith. So we can approach Him with the humble sense of our unworthiness, but also with full hope, love, and devotion—preparing a spacious tabernacle for Him in our heart. How and in what way? By banishing from our heart not only our sinful passions, but every thought of anything but the Lord.

Then, after our communion of the Holy Mysteries, let us immediately enter the secret depths of our heart and there worship the Lord with faithful humility—inwardly saying to Him something like:

You see, O my all-merciful Lord, how easily I fall into
sin, to my ruin. You also see what power the passion that
attacks me has over me—and how powerless I am to free
myself from it. Help me. Give power to my powerless
struggles. Or rather, take up my weapons Yourself and
fight for me—to overthrow my cruel enemy once and
for all.

Afterward, let us turn to the heavenly Father of our
Lord Jesus Christ and of ourselves, who together with
His Son has, in His goodness, entered into us in these
Mysteries; and to the Holy Spirit, whose grace has
inspired and prepared us for partaking of the flesh and
blood of the Lord, and who now, after Communion,
richly sheds His grace upon us; and adore the one God,
worshiped in the Holy Trinity, who bestows His favors
upon us.

Having given Him reverent thanks for the great
mercy shown us at this moment, let us present to Him
as an offering our firm resolution, readiness, and fervent
desire to fight our sin—in the hope of overcoming it by
the power of the one God in Three Persons. For consider:
if we do not give our whole heart, effort, and energy
to conquer our passions, how can we expect help from
God?

And if, in struggling with the greatest intensity
and diligence, we rely only on our own powers, we
will never succeed. We must labor with diligence, but
expect success only from God's help. Help will surely

come—and He, making our powerless efforts all-powerful, will give us an easy victory over that against which we struggle.

KINDLING LOVE FOR GOD THROUGH THE EUCHARIST

Loving God is essential for us all, but how can we help our love for Him grow? One way is through the Eucharist. In order to awaken a greater love of God in ourselves by entering deeply into the heavenly (for it is truly in heaven we celebrate the Eucharist) sacrament of the Body and Blood of Christ, we must turn our thoughts to contemplation of the love God has shown us personally in this sacrament.

We must remember our great and almighty God was not content with creating us in His image and likeness. And when we had sinned and offended Him—and consequently fallen from our high position of communion with Him—He was not satisfied with sending His only begotten Son. For His Son lived on earth thirty-three years to deliver us. Then, through terrible torment and painful death on the Cross, He redeemed us and snatched us from the hands of the devil (to whom we had become enslaved through sin), restoring us to our former position. Nor was He yet finished, for He also deigned to establish the sacrament of His Body and Blood as spiritual food for us, so the whole power of His Incarnation might permeate our entire nature. Therefore, it behooves us to make this final token of God's love for us the object of our constant contemplation and deep reflection—so that, comprehending its fullness and richness, we may feed and stimulate our heart with undivided love and longing for God.

Let us, therefore:

1) Think about when God began to love us—and when we do we will realize His love for us had no beginning. For since He is eternal in His divine nature, His love for us is also eternal. And by that love, He took counsel with Himself before all ages and resolved to give us His Son in a miraculous and indescribable manner. Realizing this, we can rejoice and say: "Even in the great expanses of eternity my insignificance was watched over and loved by the infinite God. Even then He provided for my good, and in His love—which is beyond all words—resolved to give me His Only-begotten Son for spiritual food. Knowing all this, can I permit myself even for a single moment to fail to cling to Him with all my thoughts, all my desires, and all my heart?"

2) Realize all mutual affections between creatures, however great they may be, have limits beyond which they cannot go. Only the love of God for us is limitless. So when it became necessary to satisfy it in a certain special way, He sacrificed His Son for it—His very Son who is His equal in greatness and eternity, for He shares one and the same nature. Thus the love of God is as great as His gift, and conversely, His gift is as great as His love. Both are so very great no created mind can conceive of anything greater. It is up to us to respond

to this boundless love with all the love of which we are capable.

3) Reflect further, God did not conceive His love for us through any necessity. Rather He loves us through the lovingkindness natural to Him. He loved us spontaneously, with a love as much beyond measure as it is beyond understanding.

4) Reflect also, we could never have earned this love by any deed so worthy of praise or reward that the infinite God would remedy our utter poverty with the wealth of His love. He loved us only because, in His lovingkindness, He wished it—and not only loved us, but gave Himself to us, His unworthy creatures.

5) Look at the purity of His love and see: unlike the love of humans or any other creatures, it is not mixed with any expectation of gain from outside—for He is Himself all-satisfying and all-blessed. Therefore, His wish to pour His inexpressible love and lovingkindness upon us is not for the sake of any profit for Himself, but for our good alone. Considering all this, how can we help crying out within:

> How wonderful, how marvelous! The Almighty God
> has laid His heart upon me, the least of His creatures!
> What do You wish of me, O King of glory? What do You
> expect of me—who am nothing but dust and ashes? I
> see clearly, O Lord my God, in the light of Your infinite
> love, You have but one desire, which most reveals the
> radiance of Your love for me: namely, You desire to
> give me the whole of Yourself as food and drink, for no

other reason than to transfigure the whole of me into Yourself—not because You have any need of me, but because I have extreme need of You. For in this way You dwell in me and I in You. And through this union of love I become as You are. In human words: through the union of my earthly heart with Your heavenly heart, a single godly heart is created in me.

The fact is, such thoughts cannot help filling us with wonder and joy when we see ourselves so highly valued by God and so beloved by Him—and understand, in His infinite love for us He seeks and desires nothing from us. He only wishes to attract our love to Himself, and through it to give us joy by delivering us from every attachment our passions would cause us to make to ourselves and other creatures. For then we will be able to bring the whole of ourselves as a burnt offering to Him. And for all the rest of our life, only love of Him and a fervent desire to please Him will possess our mind, our will, our memory, and all our senses.

Any and every favor springing from God's love for us can produce this effect in our soul—but it comes most naturally when we are able to look at the blessed sacrament of the Eucharist with understanding. Thus, while we consider it with our mind (recognizing we are dealing with Christ our Lord), it is good to open our heart to it, pouring out worshipful prayers such as:

O heavenly Food! When shall the hour come when I am totally consumed, not by some other fire, but by

the fire of Your love? O uncreated Love, O Bread of
Life! When shall I live by You alone, for You alone, and
in You alone? When, O my Life, wonderful, gracious
and eternal; when, O Manna from heaven, shall I turn
away from all other earthly food; when shall I desire
only You and be fed by You alone? When will it be, O
my all-satisfying goodness—O my highest good? O my
Lord, most desired and most good! Tear this poor heart
of mine from every wrong attachment and tendency.
Adorn it with Your holy virtue and fill it with that good
disposition which would make me, in all sincerity, do all
things only to please You! Then I shall at last succeed in
opening my heart to You—no longer unworthy of You—
and, petitioning You with love, get You to enter into it.
And then, my Lord, having entered my heart, You will
not meet with resistance and will perform therein all the
actions you perform in souls devoted to You.

Such loving thoughts and prayers give us a proper
way to spend the evening and the morning preparing for Communion. Then, when the sacred hour of
Communion draws near, we can envision vividly, with
humility and warmth of heart, whom we are about to
receive into ourselves—and who we are who are about
to receive Him.

He is the Son of God, clothed in inconceivable
greatness—before whom the heavens and all the powers
tremble. He is the Holy of Holies, brighter than the sun,
purity beyond all comprehension. In His love for us He
took the form of a slave, chose to be despised, scorned,

and crucified by the malice of the lawless world—and at the same time remained God, holding in His hand the life and death of the whole world. And who am I, who are you, who are we? I am nothing, insignificant—and in my corruption, evil, and malice have become less than nothing, worse than the least and most unclean of all creatures, the laughingstock of the demons of hell. Carried away by my fantasies and lusts, I have scorned my great Lord and Benefactor. And, instead of giving thanks to my generous God for so many and such great favors, I have trodden underfoot His priceless Blood—spilled for my sake.

Yet in spite of all, in His unceasing and unchanging love, He is calling me, He is calling you, He is calling us to His Divine Supper. At times He even forces us to approach it by fearful warnings, reminding us of His words to all: "Unless you eat the flesh of the Son of Man and drink His blood, you have no life in you" (John 6:53). And just as He does not shut the door of His mercy to us, so He does not turn His face away from us—even though, in our sins, we are lepers, weak, blind, and poor, slaves to all passions and vices.

The only things He demands of us are:

- that we grieve in our heart at having offended Him;
- that we abhor sin above all things—any sin, great or small;
- that we give ourselves up to Him completely and are concerned about just one thing with all the love and longing of our heart: to conform to His will always and

in everything we do, and to be forever fully obedient to
Him alone;

• that we have a firm faith in Him and an unshakable trust that He will have mercy on us, will cleanse
us from all our sins, and will protect us from all our
enemies, both visible and invisible.

Strengthened by this inexpressible love of God for
us, we may approach Holy Communion with holy fear
and love, saying:

> I am unworthy, O Lord, to receive You, for I have
> angered You by my sins many times, without number,
> and have not yet mourned for all my wicked deeds.
>
> I am unworthy, O Lord, to receive You, for I have not
> yet cleansed myself of my dispositions and attachments
> to what is not pleasing to You.
>
> I am unworthy, O Lord, to receive You, for I have not
> yet surrendered in all sincerity to Your love, Your will,
> and obedience to You.
>
> O my God, all-powerful and infinitely good: in Your
> merciful lovingkindness, make me worthy of receiving
> You, for I come to You with faith.

Then, after we have received Holy Communion, we
may shut ourselves in the secret depths of our heart, and,
forgetting all created things, pray to God in words like
these:

> O Almighty King of heaven and earth! Who made You
> enter my unworthy heart, when I am accursed, poor,

blind, and naked? No one, of course, for You came in Your immeasurable love for me. O uncreated love! What do You want of me, beggar that I am? Nothing, as I see and understand, except my love for You. Nothing, except that no other fire should burn on the altar of my heart but the fire of my love for You—which would consume all love and all desire other than bringing myself to You as a burnt offering and fragrant incense. You never desired nor sought anything else from me— and do not do so now. So hear now, O Lord, the vows of my heart. For I combine my desire with Yours—and as You have given the whole of Yourself to me, so I give the whole of myself to You, to be completely in You. I know, O Lord, this cannot be unless I renounce myself completely. It cannot be if any trace of self-love remains in me, if I harbor some sympathy or disposition toward a will of my own, thoughts of my own, or some self-catering habits of my own. Therefore, I desire and endeavor from now on to oppose myself in everything not acceptable to You, but which my soul may desire, and to compel myself to do everything pleasing to You— even if everything in me and outside me should rebel against it. In myself alone, I do not have strength enough to succeed in this. But since from now on You are with me, I daringly trust You Yourself will accomplish in me everything needed.

I aim and labor to make my heart one with Your heart. And I trust Your grace will grant me this.

I aim and labor to see nothing and to hear nothing, to think of nothing and to have sympathy with nothing

except what Your will, determined by Your commandments, leads me to and shows. And I trust it will be
granted me by Your power working in me.

I aim and endeavor not to let my attention stray
from my heart, where You dwell—there to gaze at You
unceasingly and to be warmed by the rays of light
radiating from You. And I trust this will be given me by
the touch and embrace of Your hands.

I aim and endeavor to make You alone my light,
strength, and joy from this time on. And I trust to be
given this by Your saving action on my inner being.

This is what I pray for now and shall always
continue to pray for. O merciful Lord, grant me this, I
pray.

Then we must endeavor to increase from day to day
our faith in this most holy sacrament of the Eucharist,
never ceasing to wonder at the miraculous mystery of
it, reflecting on how God manifests Himself to us in the
form of bread and wine—becoming essentially present
in us, to make us more holy, righteous, and blessed. For
the Savior Himself has said: "Blessed are those who
have not seen and yet have believed" (John 20:29). Nor
should we wish God would show Himself to us in this
life in any other form than this sacrament.

Let us try to kindle in ourselves a warm desire for this
sacrament and to make progress every day, both in our
fervent readiness to do God's will alone, and in spiritual
wisdom—making it the queen and ruler over all our
actions of the spirit, the soul, and the body. Every time

we take Communion, while partaking of this bloodless sacrifice, we are to offer ourselves a sacrifice to God. In that vein, it is good to tell Him of our total readiness to endure every affliction, every sorrow, and every wrong we may meet in the course of our life—for the sake of the love of God, who sacrificed Himself for us.

Saint Basil the Great describes more fully the duty imposed on the communicant by Holy Communion, basing his words on those of Saint Paul, saying that those who eat the Body of the Lord and drink His Blood show the Lord's death (1 Corinthians 11:26). This death was suffered by the Lord for the sake of all people—and thus for us who partake. For what purpose? "That those who live should live no longer for themselves, but for Him who died for them and rose again" (2 Corinthians 5:15). So those who approach Holy Communion with faith, love, and such readiness to be faithful to God's commandments and to every clear manifestation of His will that they are prepared to lay down their lives for it, undertake the task to live no longer either for themselves, for the world, or for sin. Instead, they undertake to live for the Lord God they receive into themselves in Holy Communion—He who died and rose again for them.

Finally, having received the Lord through Holy Communion—the Lord who sacrificed Himself for us—and having partaken of the power of this sacrifice, after glorifying the Lord and giving thanks to Him, it is also proper, in the name of this sacrifice, to offer prayers and supplications to our heavenly Father for our own needs of body, soul, and spirit; the needs of the holy Church of God; the needs of our family; the needs of those who do us good and assist us in any way; and the souls of those who have died in faith.

Being connected with the sacrifice through which the Son of God has obtained mercy for us all from God the Father, this prayer will be heard and will not be without fruit.

STUDY QUESTIONS

1. *How do you prepare yourself for Holy Communion? What do you find in this chapter you can apply to assist you in preparation?*
2. *How have you previously worked to kindle love for God within?*
3. *Of what value do you find the five steps suggested early in this chapter?*
4. *Consider the four things set forth as "the only things He demands of us." What is the most difficult of these? How can we truly do them?*
5. *What can we do to make the prayers of this chapter truly our own?*

CHAPTER 9

On Spiritual Communion and Thanksgiving to God

COMMUNION WITH THE LORD IN THE SPIRIT

Communion with the Lord through the sacrament of His Body and Blood is possible only at set times—as the schedule of the Church and our own opportunities and zeal allow. But inner communion with the Lord, in the spirit, is possible every day, every hour, and every minute. That is, through His grace it is possible to have constant inner communion with Him—and to be aware, when He so wishes, of this communion in our heart. According to the Lord's own promise, by partaking of His Body and Blood we receive Him—and He enters to dwell in us with all His blessings, allowing the heart prepared for it to be aware of His presence.

But we are constrained by the needs and limitations of our body and surrounded by those external activities and relationships in which duty calls us to take part. Thus, our attention and feeling are divided day by day, so our spiritual partaking of the Lord becomes overlaid and hidden by other things. Nevertheless, though the sense of partaking is hidden, communion with the Lord is not broken unless some sin unfortunately enters and interrupts it. Nothing can compare with the delight of this communion with the Lord, and diligent Christians, when they feel it weaken, hasten to restore its full power.

And when they have restored it, they feel themselves partaking of the Lord once more. This is spiritual communion with the Lord.

This is the way spiritual communion takes place during the time passing between our opportunities to commune with the Lord through the Holy Mysteries. And it can actually be unceasing—continual—in a person who keeps his heart pure and his attention and feeling constantly directed toward the Lord. All the same, this is a gift of grace—granted to someone struggling on the path of the Lord, if he is diligent and ruthless in controlling himself.

If we partake of the Lord in spirit only from time to time, even this partaking is a gift of grace. All we can bring is a hunger and thirst for this gift—and diligent effort to obtain it. There are, however, works which open the way to such communion with the Lord—and help us to obtain it, although it always seems to come unexpectedly. These works are: pure prayer, accompanied with childlike crying from the heart; and special acts of self-denial in the practice of virtues.

When no sin pollutes the soul, when no sinful thoughts or feelings are tolerated—that is, when the soul is pure and cries to God—what can keep the Lord, who is present, from letting that soul taste Him, or from awareness of this taste?

Thus, the soul so prepared experiences communion with the Lord and is aware of it—unless the Lord deems it better, for the good of that soul, to prolong its thirst and hunger for Him before satisfying it. Among acts of self-denial, the most powerful of all for this purpose is humble obedience and casting oneself under the feet of everyone—that is, stripping oneself of possessiveness and suffering injustice with a good spirit, all this in the spirit of complete surrender to the will of God. Such behavior makes a person more like the Lord than does any other. And the Lord, present in that person, allows his soul to taste Him. In addition, pure and diligent fulfillment of all God's commandments bears fruit: leading to the abiding of the Lord (together with the Father and the Holy Spirit) in the heart: "If anyone loves Me, he will keep My word; and My Father will love him, and We will come to him and make Our home with him" (John 14:23).

Spiritual communion with the Lord should not be confused with mental memory of having communed with Him in the Mysteries of His Body and Blood—even if this memory is accompanied by strong spiritual sensations and a fervent longing for actual Communion with Him in the Holy Mysteries once again. Neither must it be confused with what the worshipers present in the church service receive when the Eucharist is celebrated. They receive divine sanctification and compassion as participants in the bloodless sacrifice through faith, repentance, and readiness to sacrifice themselves to the glory of God. And they receive to the measure they have these inner states of mind and heart (faith, repentance, and readiness to sacrifice themselves for His glory). But even that is not the same as spiritual communion with Him—though such communion may indeed take place during the Liturgy.

ON GIVING THANKS TO THE LORD

Every blessing we obtain and every good deed we do is of God and comes from God. It is, therefore, our duty to give thanks to Him for everything: for every blessing we receive from His generous hand, whether visible or invisible, for every right action, for every right effort, and for every victory over the enemies of our salvation, as the Scriptures direct: "In everything give thanks; for this is the will of God in Christ Jesus for you" (1 Thessalonians 5:18).

So we must take care to maintain feelings of gratitude to God—feelings kept warm from the moment we awake in the morning, throughout the day, and as the inspiration for words of thanks on our lips as we go to sleep. For throughout our days and nights we are immersed in divine blessings—one of which is sleep itself.

We must remember: God does not need our thanks, but we stand in extreme need of divine blessings. And the place to receive and store these blessings is a grateful heart. "The best way of preserving the benevolence of a benefactor," says Saint John Chrysostom, "is remembrance of his favor and constantly giving thanks."

And Saint Isaac the Syrian writes, "The gratitude of the receiver encourages the giver to bestow greater gifts than before. A person who is not grateful for little will be disappointed in hopes of much. A gift is always increased except when there is no gratitude."

Saint Basil the Great adds a useful warning:

> If we do not give thanks for the blessings given by God, it becomes necessary to withdraw these blessings in order to bring us to our senses. As the eyes fail to see what is too near, but need a suitable distance, so ungrateful souls, when deprived of blessings, often become aware of former mercies. And while they had no gratitude to the Giver when they enjoyed the gifts, they glorify the past when they have lost it (chapter on giving thanks, p. 74, Vol. 4).

But what does it take to make us thankful—how can we fire up the proper feelings of gratitude in ourselves and always keep them? We can start by examining all of God's favors to mankind—to our race in general—and to ourselves in particular, going over them frequently in our thoughts, rehearsing them in our memory. If we have a heart, we will not be able to refrain from singing our thanksgiving to God as a result. Examples of such thanksgiving may be found in the prayers and services of the Church and in the writings of the saints. Saint Basil the Great, for instance, describes God's generosity toward us in this manner:

> We were brought from nonexistence into being, were created in the image of the Creator, were endowed with mind and speech which constitute the perfection of our nature and give us knowledge of God. Under diligent

study, the beauties of creation are like a book showing us
the greatness of God's Providence in all things—and His
Wisdom. We can discern good from evil. Nature itself
teaches us to choose what is useful and turn away from
the harmful. Being estranged from God by sin, we are
recalled to communion with Him, freed from shameful
and humiliating slavery by the blood of His Only-
begotten Son. And what shall we say of the hope of
salvation and the delights of angelic bliss—and what
of the kingdom of heaven and the promised blessings,
surpassing all word or understanding! (ibid., p. 51).

We may read this description of God's favors toward
us or choose another—even compose our own, including in it the blessings which God has given us personally. Then repeat them often in word or thought, not
only every day, but many times a day. If we do, we will
always have feelings of gratitude to God.

Once aroused, however, a feeling does not like to
stay hidden: it seeks a way to reveal and express itself.
So how can we appropriately express our feelings of
gratitude to God? First, by doing what He wants us to
do when He surrounds us with His abundant gifts. And
what does He want?

• Surrounding us with His blessings, God desires
that, seeing them, we constantly remember Him. So let
us remember.

• He wants us to cling to Him wholeheartedly with
love. So let us cling to Him.

• He wants us never to stray from His will in

anything we do: to endeavor to please Him in every way. So let us give ourselves over to striving to please Him.

• He wants us to rely upon Him alone in all things. So let us trust Him in everything.

• He wants us to love and care for our neighbors as ourselves.

• He wants us to do our work with thankful hearts.

• He wants us to remember the many occasions on which we have offended Him, our true Benefactor, by our wicked and shameful deeds, so we are filled with true remorse of conscience, repent and weep until we make peace with our conscience and receive the assurance God has completely forgiven us. So let us do this.

Thus, we see how very wide the field of thanksgiving is to be—and how many means are available to fulfill this duty. From this we learn how unpardonable is the sin of those who neglect to do so. And we must also learn to work diligently not to stain ourselves with this sin. Ungratefulness is a dark and terrible sin—terrible enough we cannot find words to express the extent of its failure.

Let us, therefore, take care always to keep the feelings of gratitude to God warm within ourselves—especially in church during the Liturgy of the Eucharist—for the word "Eucharist" means giving thanks. And let us not forget: the only worthy thanks we can offer to God is complete readiness to sacrifice ourselves and all we have to the glory of His Holy Name.

STUDY QUESTIONS

1. *What is necessary in order to experience communion with the Lord in the spirit?*
2. *How can you go about preparing yourself for the type of communion described in this chapter?*
3. *How have you formed the habit of giving thanks to the Lord? What value do you see in the regular, even constant, giving of thanks to Him?*
4. *What do you find in this chapter which you can apply directly to your own prayer life?*

INDEX

A

absolution   54, 104–105
abstinence   64. *See also* fasting
almsgiving.   *See* giving
angels   17, 26, 77, 85, 94, 99
anxiety   71
Ascension of Christ   60, 81, 92, 101
Athanasius, St.   64
attention
  in prayer   21–25, 35, 38, 41, 46, 48, 49
  to one's spiritual condition   56–57, 71, 120, 123–124
attitudes needed for prayer   11–20
avarice   58

B

baptism   6–7, 54, 82, 97, 103, 105
Basil the Great, St.   15, 127, 130
  Liturgy of   102
blessings   11, 13, 15, 19, 33, 123, 126–130
  obtained through prayer   11, 18, 21
body   29, 53, 81, 120
  discipline of   51
  needs of   16, 123
Body of Christ (the Church)   75–76, 78, 90–106
bowing in prayer   41, 49
bread, daily   85–86

C

Callistus, St.   49
Canonicon   24
chrismation   103, 105
Christ   33, 43, 44, 57–59, 72, 83, 98, 115
  as High Priest   69, 93, 94, 96
  Body and Blood of   91–107, 112–123, 125
  calling on   58
  commitment to   6–7, 84
  faith in   33

Christ (cont.)
  forgiveness of   87, 104
  life in   64, 84, 86, 97
  partaking of   92
  present in the Eucharist   62, 92–93, 94, 111, 116
  receiving inwardly   91–92
  suffering of   109
  unity in   99, 100
  work of   16
Christian living   52
Chrysostom, St. John. *See* John Chrysostom, St.
Church
  attending   52
  corporate worship of   72–73, 75–76, 90–106
  fasting in   61–67
  giving in   68–69
  mystery of   90, 94, 104
  prayers of   24, 25, 76, 127
  unity of   95, 98–99
commandments   15, 55, 65, 94, 104, 106, 108, 120, 121, 125
communion
  with God   100, 106, 108, 123–130, 128. *See also* union with
    God
  with the Church   100–101
Communion, Holy. *See* Eucharist
compassion   30, 64, 72, 125
confession of sin   15, 21, 54, 86–88, 104–105, 107
conscience   15, 129
consciousness of God   38, 42
contemplation   22, 27, 36, 113
Cornelius   60
Cross of Christ   16, 101, 110, 112
Cyprian of Carthage, St.   81, 83–84, 104

D
daydreaming   65
death   31, 48, 99
  of Christ   16, 52, 60, 97, 109, 110, 112, 121
demons   58–59, 60
devil   56, 58, 84, 112. *See also* enemy, the

discipline of the body   51
distraction   39, 52

E
ecstasy   24
emotion   24
enemies   15, 37, 56, 108–109, 118, 126
enemy, the   56–57, 91–92, 111. *See also* devil
entertainment   52, 65
Ephraim the Syrian, St.   42
Eucharist   90–106, 107–122, 125, 129
   preparation for   107–112

F
faith   12–13, 16, 22, 30, 33, 110, 118, 125
family   51, 78, 122
fantasies   58, 65
fasting
   definition of   64–67
   history of   60
   proper attitude in   63
   purpose of   61
   relationship of to prayer   60–64, 71
   rules of   64
Father, God as   44, 46, 77, 79–80, 80–82, 111, 121, 125
Fathers, Holy. *See* Holy Fathers
father, spiritual. *See* spiritual father
fear of God   22, 53, 69, 87, 118
feelings, prayerful   19, 22, 27
fiction   52
flesh   51, 56, 85
food   51, 63, 64, 116
   spiritual   61, 62, 86, 94, 95, 112–115
forgiveness   86–88, 105, 129
fornication   65
fruit of prayer   18, 23, 27, 122

G
generosity of God   127–130
giving, relationship of to prayer   60, 64, 67–76

glorifying God   15, 81, 121
glory of God   15, 26–27, 31, 72, 83, 107, 125, 129
gluttony   65–66
good deeds. *See* works
goodness of God   11, 12, 15, 87, 111
gossip   65
grace   14, 22, 33, 37, 45, 47–48, 53–55, 69, 72, 80, 82, 85, 91, 95, 103, 111, 119, 123, 124
gratitude   15, 72, 110, 126–130. *See also* thanksgiving
greed   71
Gregory of Sinai, St.   49, 57

H
heart
  devoted to God   13, 67, 71, 107–111, 113, 115 –117, 119, 123, 127
  guarding   38–39
  prayer of   21–23, 49, 54, 55
  purity of   73, 86, 124
  role of in prayer   21–23, 23–24, 35–36, 72, 78, 118, 124
  warmth of   116
heaven   71, 79–81, 84–85, 92–94, 99, 112. *See also* Kingdom of heaven
hell   87
help from God   12, 15, 16, 18, 25, 29, 33, 42, 47, 56–57, 85, 108, 111
Hesychius, St.   42, 61
Hilary of Poitiers, St.   82
holiness   82, 83, 85, 120
Holy Fathers   8, 17, 36, 39, 40, 45–50, 65–67
Holy Spirit   33–34, 66, 81, 95, 97, 111, 125. *See also* Spirit, Holy
  helps us to pray   25, 32
  in prayer   22, 25, 32
Holy Trinity   24–25, 42, 44, 48, 75, 77, 96–98, 111
hope in God   22, 30, 42, 47, 90, 109, 110
humility   17, 45, 46, 49, 65–67, 72, 83, 110, 116
hunger
  for God   124
  for righteousness   80

I

Ignatius, St.   49
ill-will   58
improvisation in prayer   32, 77
Incarnation of Christ   12, 15, 36, 52, 71, 90, 107, 112
individualism   78, 98
individuality   26
ingratitude   110, 129
intercession   16–17, 25, 57, 100
Isaac of Syria, St.   42, 130

J

Jesus Prayer   42–45, 53, 54
Joannicius, St.   42, 47
John Cassian, St.   40, 42
John Chrysostom, St.   19, 41, 42, 66, 130
   Liturgy of   97–98
John Climacus, St.   69
John of Damascus, St.   26
John of the Ladder, St.   42, 48
judgment   87

K

Kingdom of heaven   33, 69, 71, 80, 82, 83–84, 103, 128

L

Last Supper   90, 93–94
Liturgy   93–106, 126, 129
Lord's Prayer   60, 78, 79
love
   for God   22, 71, 72, 87, 110, 125, 128
   for neighbor   51, 64, 72, 97–98, 100, 129
   of God for us   11, 26, 44, 55, 112–122, 125
   of pleasure   83
lust   51, 56, 58, 65, 110, 117

M

Macarius of Egypt, St.   53
Maximus the Confessor, St.   14
meditation   25, 44, 52

mercy   12, 15, 17, 33, 40, 42, 54, 72, 85, 87, 110, 111, 117, 118, 122
mind   13, 23, 27, 28, 31, 53, 58, 62, 97, 107, 115, 125, 127
  in prayer   21–23, 31, 36, 43, 66
money   68–76
Mother of God   17, 54
Mystery of the Eucharist. *See* Eucharist

N
Name of God   15, 24, 31, 58, 74, 80, 82, 83, 129
needs, expressing in prayer   16, 21, 26, 35–36, 41, 121
Nicephorus the Monk, St.   49

O
obedience to God's will   13, 20, 33, 53, 71, 118, 125

P
parable of the unjust judge   17
passions   16, 56, 58, 84, 108, 109, 110, 115, 117
patience   13, 17, 18, 19, 30, 32, 50
perfection
  attaining   16, 37, 39, 47
  of God   12, 36, 108
persistence in prayer   17–19
petition   18, 26, 27, 85, 116
Philokalia   49, 55, 57–59, 66
pleasing God   14, 15, 17, 19, 53, 115, 116, 118, 119, 129
praise   12, 15, 21, 26
prayer
  always heard   18–19
  as weapon in spiritual warfare   11, 90
  attitudes needed for   11–20
  constant   22, 39
  corporate   74, 75–76, 101, 105–106
  four elements of   15
  goal of   72
  in our own words   35–36
  inner   21–33, 38
  mental   21–33

prayer (cont.)
   persistence in   17–19
   personal   74, 75–76, 105–106
   preparation for   29
   real   21, 37, 38, 53, 55–57
   rule of   31, 35, 39, 41, 42, 43, 47, 53, 75, 77
   success in   28–32, 45, 49, 51–53, 111
   sudden impulses to   36–38
   training in   23–24
   with the heart   21–33, 37–38
   with the spirit   21–33, 37
   with words   21–33
   working at   51–53
prayer books   24–25
prayers
   evening   24–25
   Jesus Prayer. *See* Jesus Prayer
   Lord's Prayer. *See* Lord's Prayer
   memorizing   28
   morning   24–25
   of Chrysostom, 24 short   41
   printed in text   15, 111, 114, 115, 118
   short   40–41, 42–45
   written   35–36
presence of God   22, 29, 32, 33, 36, 38, 42, 45, 46, 48, 68, 75, 81, 91, 92, 94, 120, 123–126
pride   37, 43, 65–67, 71
priest
   role of in confession   104
   role of in the Eucharist   96
Providence, divine   20, 36, 101, 108, 128
psalms   35, 40–42, 47

R
reading   52
redemption   12, 24, 71, 94, 100–103, 103
religions, Eastern   44
repentance   15, 21, 22, 46, 53, 54, 60, 104–105, 107, 110, 125, 129
repetition of the Jesus Prayer   47–50

requests in prayer   14, 26, 30
resentment   87–88
rest   51, 56, 99
resurrection   64, 100
Resurrection of Christ   60, 92, 99, 101
rule of prayer. *See* prayer: rule of

S

sacraments   90, 103–104. *See also* confession of sin
sacrifice
   of Christ   93–94, 113, 121, 125
   readiness to make   22, 121, 125, 129
saints   17, 77, 94, 100, 127
salvation   15, 33, 52–54, 56, 80, 83, 86, 101, 105, 126, 128
sanctification   83, 125
Scriptures   8, 36, 62, 103, 105, 126
self-centeredness   26, 78
self-control   65–67, 124
self-denial   124
self-examination   104
selfishness   51, 81, 98
self-love   13, 119
senses   52, 81, 93, 115
service
   to God   11–12, 12, 14, 67, 71, 106, 107, 110
   to others   51, 53, 106
sign of the Cross   24
Simeon the New Theologian, St.   49
sin   12, 15, 21, 42, 52, 62, 65, 66, 72, 75, 83, 84, 86–
      88, 90, 94, 107–112, 117–118, 121, 123, 124, 128, 129. *See
      also* confession of sin
sleep   51, 126
soul   32, 35, 46, 53, 56, 58, 61, 62, 120, 122, 124
   needs of   16
spirit   21, 22, 27, 29, 31, 38, 40, 46, 56, 85, 91, 120, 123, 124
   in the heart   38–39, 46, 48
   needs of   16
   of prayer   25, 31, 36, 37
   role of in prayer   11, 21–23, 23–24
Spirit, Holy   13. *See also* Holy Spirit

spiritual concentration   24–25
spiritual father   5, 45, 47–50, 54, 64, 77, 104–105, 107
spiritual warfare. *See* warfare, spiritual
supplication   26, 81, 121

T
television   52, 65
temples of God   80
tempting God   14
thanksgiving   15–17, 19, 21, 26–27, 29, 101, 111, 126–130
thoughts
   evil   57
   of God   38
throne of God   23
tithing   67
training in prayer   23–24
Trinity, Holy. *See* Holy Trinity
trust in God   11, 13, 18, 53, 118, 119, 129

U
union with God   26, 46, 91, 92, 108–109, 112, 115
unjust judge, parable of. *See* parable of the unjust judge
unseen warfare   55–57. *See also* warfare, spiritual

V
vain repetitions   43
virtue   14, 16, 33, 61, 62, 66, 109, 116, 124

W
walking before God   22
warfare, spiritual   59
   role of prayer in   55–57
   weapons for   11, 55–57, 90–92
widow and unjust judge   17
will
   of God   13–14, 16, 22, 29, 53, 56, 62, 71, 72, 84–85, 110,
      117, 118, 119, 120, 121, 125, 126, 128
   our own   13–14, 53, 115
works   106, 126
   and faith   72

works (cont.)
  and fasting   64
  and prayer   14, 52, 124
  and salvation   33
world
  cares of   24, 71
  contact with   51–52
  enticements of   39, 56
  renouncing   84, 121
worship   12, 26, 67, 70–72, 76, 90–106, 110–122

Z
zeal   12, 53, 54, 56, 80, 123

Companion Volumes to
Prayer in the Unseen Warfare:

- ***Victory in the Unseen Warfare***
  ISBN 978-0-9622713-6-6

- ***Virtue in the Unseen Warfare***
  ISBN 978-0-9622713-8-0

The three books in the series—
Victory, Virtue, and Prayer—
are complementary in content but do not overlap.
They can be read separately or as a series.

Other books available from Ancient Faith Publishing

Thirty Steps to Heaven
The Ladder of Divine Ascent for All Walks of Life
by Archimandrite Vassilios Papavassiliou

Many laypeople have attempted to read the great spiritual classic, *The Ladder of Divine Ascent,* but have been frustrated in attempting to apply the lessons of this monastic text in their everyday lives in the world. Archimandrite Vassilios interprets the *Ladder* for the ordinary Christian without sacrificing any of its beauty and power. Now you too can accept the challenge offered by St. John Climacus to ascend closer to God with each passing day.

Meditations for Great Lent
Reflections on the Triodion
by Archimandrite Vassilios Papavassiliou

The Lenten Triodion exhorts us, "Let us observe a fast acceptable and pleasing to the Lord." Using hymns from the Triodion and the Scripture readings appointed for the season, *Meditations for Great Lent* shows us how to make our fast acceptable: to fast not only from food but from sin; to fast with love and humility, as a means to an end and not an end in itself. Keep this gem of a book with you to inspire you for the Fast and to dip into for encouragement as you pursue your Lenten journey.

Meditations for Holy Week
Dying and Rising with Christ
by Archimandrite Vassilios Papavassiliou

Archimandrite Vassilios brings his liturgical and devotional insights and warm, accessible style to bear on the services of Holy Week, helping the reader enter fully into this most rich and intense period of the Christian year.

Meditations for Advent
Preparing for Christ's Birth
by Archimandrite Vassilios Papavassiliou

The author of *Meditations for Great Lent* takes us through the hymnography, Scripture readings, and iconography for the forty days leading up to the Nativity of Christ, showing how a full understanding of the Incarnation can enrich our spiritual lives.

Bread & Water, Wine & Oil
by Archimandrite Meletios Webber

According to two thousand years of experience, Orthodoxy shows us how to be transformed by the renewing of our mind—a process that is aided by participation in the traditional ascetic practices and Mysteries of the Church. In this unique and accessible book, Archimandrite Meletios Webber first explores the role of mystery in the Christian life, then walks the reader through the seven major Mysteries of the Orthodox Church, showing the way to a richer, fuller life in Christ.

The Scent of Holiness
by Constantina Palmer

Every monastery exudes the scent of holiness, but women's monasteries have their own special flavor. Join Constantina Palmer as she makes frequent pilgrimages to a women's monastery in Greece and absorbs the nuns' particular approach to their spiritual life. If you're a woman who's read of Mount Athos and longed to partake of its grace-filled atmosphere, this book is for you. Men will find it a fascinating read as well.

Turning the Heart to God
by St. Theophan the Recluse

One of the most profound works on repentance in all of Christendom. St. Theophan, a beloved Orthodox bishop from nineteenth-century Russia, speaks not only from a deep knowledge of the Church Fathers, but also from a lifetime of experience in turning his heart to God—and guiding others on this glorious Way that leads to our salvation.

A Beginner's Guide to Spirituality:
The Orthodox Path to a Deeper Relationship with God
by Fr. Michael Keiser

Spirituality is in! Monks go platinum with recordings of chant, and books on self-help spirituality overflow supermarket bookracks. But what is the meaning of true spirituality? Aren't we all a little confused? Genuine spirituality keeps us in balance with God, our neighbor, and the material world. Fr. Michael Keiser walks us through the Orthodox Church's timeless teachings and practices on the ancient understanding of Christian spirituality with humor and keen insight. He outlines how ascetic practices, personal and corporate worship, confession and repentance, overcoming the passions, and opening ourselves up to God's grace can lead us to transformation, and to our ultimate destiny—Jerusalem, the heavenly city.

All titles available at store.ancientfaith.com. Most also available as ebooks.

Ancient Faith Publishing hopes you have enjoyed and benefited from this book. The proceeds from the sales of our books only partially cover the costs of operating our nonprofit ministry—which includes both the work of **Ancient Faith Publishing** and the work of **Ancient Faith Radio.** Your financial support makes it possible to continue this ministry both in print and online. Donations are tax-deductible and can be made at www.ancient faith.com.

To request a catalog of other publications,
please call us at (800) 967-7377 or (219) 728-2216
or log onto our website: **store.ancientfaith.com**

Bringing you Orthodox Christian music, readings, prayers,
teaching, and podcasts 24 hours a day since 2004 at
www.ancientfaith.com

CPSIA information can be obtained
at www.ICGtesting.com
Printed in the USA
LVHW01s1426120817
544791LV00008B/13/P

9 781888 212037